The Renaissance
SECOND EDITION

ALISON BROWN

Longman

An imprint of Pearson Education

Harlow, England · London · New York · Reading, Massachusetts · San Francisco
Toronto · Don Mills, Ontario · Sydney · Tokyo · Singapore · Hong Kong · Seoul
Taipei · Cape Town · Madrid · Mexico City · Amsterdam · Munich · Paris · Milan

Pearson Education Limited,
Edinburgh Gate,
Harlow,
Essex CM20 2JE,
England.
and Associated Companies throughout the world.

Visit us on the World Wide Web at:
www.pearsoned.co.uk

First published by Longman Group 1988
This Second Edition published 1999 by Pearson Education Limited

ISBN 978-0-582-30781-0

British Library Cataloguing-in-Publication Data
A catalogue record for this book is available from the British Library.

Library of Congress Cataloging-in-Publication Data
A catalog record for this book is available.

Set by 7 in 10/12 Sabon
Printed and bound in Great Britain by Clays Ltd, Bungay, Suffolk

CONTENTS

AN INTRODUCTION TO THE SERIES

Such is the pace of historical enquiry in the modern world that there is an ever-widening gap between the specialist article or monograph, incorporating the results of current research, and general surveys, which inevitably become out of date. *Seminar Studies in History* are designed to bridge this gap. The series was founded by Patrick Richardson in 1966 and his aim was to cover major themes in British, European and World history. Between 1980 and 1996 Roger Lockyer continued his work, before handing the editorship over to Clive Emsley and Gordon Martel. Clive Emsley is Professor of History at the Open University, while Gordon Martel is Professor of International History at the University of Northern British Columbia, Canada and Senior Research Fellow at De Montfort University.

All the books are written by experts in their field who are not only familiar with the latest research but have often contributed to it. They are frequently revised, in order to take account of new information and interpretations. They provide a selection of documents to illustrate major themes and provoke discussion, and also a guide to further reading. The aim of *Seminar Studies* is to clarify complex issues without over-simplifying them, and to stimulate readers into deepening their knowledge and understanding of major themes and topics.

NOTE ON REFERENCING SYSTEM

Readers should note that numbers in square brackets [5] refer them to the corresponding entry in the Bibliography at the end of the book (specific page numbers are given in italics). A number in square brackets preceded by *Doc.* [*Doc. 5*] refers readers to the corresponding item in the Documents section which follows the main text.

ACKNOWLEDGEMENTS

The publishers would like to thank Creighton E. Gilbert for permission to reproduce extracts from his book *Italian Art 1400–1500*.

The author would like to thank Robert Black and Jonathan Nelson for kindly reading relevant chapters with suggestions for the revised edition.

PART ONE: INTRODUCTION

1 THE PROBLEM OF INTERPRETATION

'If we are to call any age golden, it must be our age which has produced such a wealth of golden intellects ... and all this in Florence'
[*Doc. 1*]. Of all the images of the Renaissance, this image of a golden
age in Florence is the most seductive. It is also the way most people
idealised the Renaissance until quite recently. In listing as his golden
people the poets, writers and artists who revived subjects that had
been forgotten or neglected in his day, Marsilio Ficino was contributing to the idea of the Renaissance as 'a revival of classical antiquity' –
the revival of subjects like poetry, history and drama, architecture and
painting, that had been studied in Ancient Greece and Rome but not
in the Middle Ages.

Not long ago, we would have considered Ficino's letter first-hand
evidence for describing the Renaissance as a dynamic period of revival
– a period when 'life reeked with joy', as one student has described it. But
few historians would now interpret it uncritically as evidence of an
optimistic new birth. Instead, they would call it a piece of publicity, or
propaganda, written to praise not only Florence (Ficino was writing
to a German, albeit a famous astronomer and intellectual) but also the
Medici family, who were his own patrons and helped to promote this
cultural revival.

The same can be said about an even more influential account of the
Renaissance, *The Lives of the Most Excellent Painters, Sculptors and
Architects* by Giorgio Vasari (1511–74) [27] and [*Doc. 4*]. Written in
the middle of the sixteenth century, Vasari's *Lives* provides us with
full and lively biographies of all the Italian artists at work during the
Renaissance. Starting 'from small beginnings' with painters like
Cimabue and Giotto in the thirteenth and fourteenth centuries 'to
reach the heights' with Michelangelo in the sixteenth, it is still the
most-quoted source of evidence about these artists today. But since
Vasari was a painter and architect in the Medici court, he could – like
Ficino – be suspected of bias in praising the Renaissance largely in
terms of Tuscan achievements – a bias that recent books like Evelyn

Welch's *Art and Society in Italy, 1350–1500* [157] works hard to counteract in describing workshops and contexts throughout Italy instead of individuals clustering around Florence.

In describing the arts as human bodies, which 'are born, grow, become old and die', Vasari also encouraged the idea of the Renaissance as a process of inevitable progress and decline. This was an idea that appealed to later writers, especially in the nineteenth century – like Jacob Burckhardt, discussed below – when people wanted to trace the origins of their newly-won freedoms and secularism; but no longer today. Surely the arts are not like human bodies: now we are much more likely to think that they are subject to the changing whims of fashion, not to nature's deterministic cycle.

For these reasons, writers like Ficino and Vasari are no longer accepted as reliable sources for describing the Renaissance. Far from being valuable witnesses of the revival, they now seem like prejudiced salesmen of a movement that appears to be 'receding from us, becoming more alien every year', as one historian has recently put it [45 *p. 210*]. Strictly speaking, this is of course true. It is also anachronistic to see the Renaissance as 'modern' according to our scale of values, as the Swiss historian Jacob Burckhardt did in his path-breaking book, *The Civilisation of the Renaissance in Italy*. Burckhardt, whose book was published (in German) in Basel in 1860, was also the first person to attempt to define the Renaissance as a historical period that involved all aspects of Italian life at the time – political and social as well as cultural. His book is a classic which even today provides the starting-point for anyone studying the Renaissance. But because of its scale and richness, it is easy to overlook the implicit value-judgements it contains about progress, 'civilisation' and Renaissance individualism [44 *pp. 81, 84, 104*].

To illustrate this, we can look at a book about the Renaissance by the English woman-writer and novelist Vernon Lee, written some twenty years after Burckhardt was first published and soon after its first English translation. 'While in the rest of Europe', she writes in *Euphorion* (London, 1885), 'men were floundering among the stagnant ideas and crumbling institutions of the effete Middle Ages with but a vague half-consciousness of their own nature, the Italians walked calmly through a life as well arranged as their great towns, bold, inquisitive and sceptical' (*p. 28*). By acting as a conduit for transmitting Burckhardt's ideas to England, she helps to explain not only his influence on the way we still see the Renaissance but also why it seems so outdated today. Not only would medievalists feel aggrieved by her account of the

Middle Ages as effete, but anyone would dislike the assumptions on which her generalisation is based.

Underlying this is another criticism of Burckhardt, and that is his idea of the Renaissance as all-embracing. According to Ernst Gombrich, it is dangerous to assume that its spirit (*Zeitgeist*) influenced every aspect of life at the time, when in fact we know that a large part of the population was totally unaffected by the new ideas. For this reason he would prefer to describe it as a cultural fashion that caught on – a return in art, for example, to primitive simplicity after the richness of the florid International Gothic style, like the later Pre-Raphaelite or Fauvist movements. His criticism stimulated a debate in the 1960s and 1970s about the Renaissance as a movement rather than a period and the extent to which it differed from earlier and later classical revivals [78; 80; 150].

In the last ten years the debate has developed in different directions. Emphasis on patronage has helped to undermine the importance of artists and writers in creating the Renaissance: more important than their individual talent were the patrons – institutional and private – who commissioned and paid for their work [100]. At the same time, other limitations of Renaissance individualism were pointed out by gender historians and historians of popular culture – like Joan Kelley, who challenged Burckhardt in a now famous article, 'Did women have a Renaissance?' [96]. Whereas he thought the classical revival encouraged equality between educated, upper-class men and women, in fact it did quite the opposite, Kelly argued, by re-introducing gender differences and reinforcing male supremacy in the sphere of culture as well as politics. He also leaves too much out of his apparently all-embracing description of the Renaissance – too many ordinary people, with deep-rooted superstitions and religious beliefs that were remarkably impervious to the new ideas. Books like *The War of the Fists* in Venice [61], *Words and Deeds in Renaissance Rome* [54] and the essays in the recent volume *Gender and Society in Renaissance Italy* [40] attempt to recover the voices of these ordinary people by describing their lives on the streets and their gender relationships, together making the highly literate culture of the Renaissance seem increasingly elitist and remote from the interests of most people then and now.

This criticism has been reinforced by the use of post-structuralist techniques to 'deconstruct' Renaissance language and reveal its ambiguities and uncertainties – as Patricia Simons explains in her model study of Renaissance portraiture [141]. They also help us to understand much better the underlying political and social function of Renaissance ideas and images, which acted not only as a source of inspiration but also as power structures, or 'systems of representation'. All these approaches, reflecting the dominant models or 'paradigms' of explanation from the 1960s to the 1980s, Marxism, the 'Annales School' and post-structuralism, have provided useful ways of understanding the limitations and the bias of Renaissance texts, teaching us how to read them more critically. And they in turn have encouraged a more open, consumerist approach to the Renaissance, which adopts the non-evaluative language of commerce to explain the circulation of Renaissance ideas as an interactive, two-way process of exchange.

Is there a danger that in pursuing these paradigms, we are losing sight of the historical Renaissance, a cultural movement firmly rooted in the social and political structures of the period? Here it may be useful to compare this cultural movement with a parallel development in the Church. Writing about an important theological shift that took place between the fourteenth and sixteenth centuries, the French historian Michel De Certeau explains it in terms of historical and anthropological changes – the break-up of old social networks and the growth of a new specialised elite ('and new conceptual models to make it thinkable'), which in turn helped to marginalise those excluded from it. The Church's attempt to re-exert control and reintegrate society through the use of visual techniques – 'showing in order to inspire belief', targeted sermons using images and exemplars, the 'monstrance' or display of the Host, exorcisms and miracles enacted and depicted – paralleled that of secular authorities involved in the same process [63 *pp. 85–7*]. From this point of view, classical culture not only offered a 'conceptual model to make [the new elite's status] thinkable', it also offered a visual language of imposing classicising forms and images to make its effect in public and private spaces – in government palaces and squares, in churches, in theatres and in private homes.

To anchor the Renaissance in this way through its social and political roots is not to deprive it of the element of excitement and novelty that still emanates from the writings of Renaissance people themselves, when they describe their passion for books, their love of Ovid 'as a kind of door and teacher', their admiration for Brunelleschi's immense dome, 'broad enough to cover all the people of Tuscany with its shadow'. The novelties of the period included the rediscovery of lost texts, like Lucretius's *On Nature of Things*, ancient statues, and the paintings in Nero's *Golden House*, as well as genuinely new discoveries, such as the inventions of gunpowder and printing, and the discovery of the 'new-found' lands in America. And even its prejudices and silences – marginalised 'barbarians' and dangerous texts that were recovered but suppressed – are useful in balancing the humanists' own high-brow view of themselves. So when writers and artists called their period new, or re-born, and the preceding period dead, they were not simply recycling an old theme but were expressing genuine belief in its novelty, frightening though they sometimes found it.

Clearly, the Renaissance is not dead either – if anything, it is more alive as a subject than it was when I last wrote about it. This is why I was persuaded to return to this book after ten years. I have revised it, not by restricting it simply to an account of the classical revival, nor, like one recent book [101], by simply expanding it to include topics of current interest that Burckhardt excluded, but by describing the Renaissance as an integrated and self-constructed movement. Like the Enlightenment, it was a movement that represented a 'capsule' of values and concerns regarded by its protagonists as progressive, in being based on reason and light in place of superstition and darkness [120]. The Renaissance, too, is difficult to describe as an all-encompassing period, confined by certain dates and places; but although the emphasis and pace were different in different places, a similar process of interaction took place between these ideas and the social and political structures of late medieval–early modern Europe, giving the period coherence from this point of view.

To explore the ideas encapsulated in this Renaissance pill or package, I follow the same trajectory as before, discussing its name and the context in which it developed before going on to describe its ingredients and its impact. Although Florence is in many ways the 'well-equipped laboratory' [as it has been called: 100 *p. 3*] that experimented with many of these ingredients – and so remains central to this book – we can no longer regard it as unique in its achievement, especially in the light of recent studies of court culture at this time. It is also in response to the new direction Renaissance studies have taken since 1992, that I give more attention to those excluded from this culture, as its other, 'dark' face, and to consumerist expansion and the exploration of new spaces. The bibliography has been updated and two new texts have been added. Otherwise, respecting the strict confines of this *Seminar Studies* series and my own understanding of what the Renaissance was about, I retain the same thematic approach as before – that is, pursuing the thread of interest and excitement in these new discoveries as a guide to a critical understanding of the outlook and mentality of this dynamic period.

2   THE CONCEPT OF REVIVAL

There is nothing new about the idea of 'rebirth', although the word 'renaissance' was scarcely used until the early nineteenth century. Christianity itself had popularised the concept of rebirth through the ritual of baptism which created a 'born-again' person with a new, Christian name. Cicero had already used the word *renovatio* to describe the Stoic theory of the cyclical destruction of the world by fire and its regeneration or rebirth (*De natura deorum* II, 46, 118); and throughout the Middle Ages this word remained in use. So when Petrarch (1304–74) suggested the dawn of a new period in the four-teenth century as men 'broke through the darkness' to 'return to the pure, pristine radiance' of antiquity, it was not in itself a novel idea. What was new was that this time it caught on and became the battle-cry for a widespread reform movement.

Soon after Petrarch talked about the dawn of a new period, his friend Giovanni Boccaccio (1313–75) described how the painter Giotto (*c.* 1266–1337) had 'brought back to the light that art that had been buried for many generations' and, elsewhere, how Dante had 'restored to life' the dead art of poetry. After Petrarch's own death, Boccaccio praised him in turn for bringing back the Muses to their 'pristine beauty', 'reviving in noble spirits the hope that had almost died ... that the way to Parnassus is open and its summit accessible'. By the fifteenth century the idea of rebirth was becoming common-place to describe the cultural revival in Italy at that time, as writers and artists in turn joined a growing list of men who contributed to a rebirth of the lost arts of painting, sculpture, architecture and litera-ture [*Doc. 2*].

The idea of rebirth was accompanied by a new periodisation of his-tory. As Robert Black has said, the concept of the Renaissance pre-supposes a historical scheme: 'for there to be rebirth, there must have been birth followed by death' [34 *p. 51*]. Although there were many different schemes that survived into the Middle Ages, some dividing history into four ages, others into six, there was a fundamental contrast between the classical belief in revolving cycles of history (condemned by St Augustine) and Christian chronology which firmly separated the period before Christ (BC) and after Christ (AD, Anno Domini, or 'in the year of Our Lord'). Petrarch first suggested the idea of a rebirth and referred to the period between classical and modern times as 'the dark ages', but it was the fifteenth-century historian, Flavio Biondo (1392–1463), who first called it the *medium aevum* or middle age. Initially there was little agreement on how long this dark period lasted – one humanist, Domenico Bandini of Arezzo (*c*. 1335–1418), suggested only one hundred years, from the twelfth-century revival to his own day, whereas for Leonardo Bruni (*c*. 1370–1444), it lasted seven hundred years, from the fall of the Roman Empire to the revival of self-governing Italian city-states in the twelfth century. By the middle of the fifteenth century, it was generally agreed that it lasted for a thousand years, from the fall of Rome in 412 until 1412.

The adjectives used by the humanists to describe the contrast between the preceding period and their own reveal their prejudices: 'barbarian', 'gross' and 'dark' for the middle period; 'civilised', 'refined' and 'light' for their own. Initially, as we have seen, their language was taken as evidence of progress. Later, it was described as myth-making: 'a legend,' C. S. Lewis wrote, which 'we have simply inherited from the people themselves' [in 38 *p. 12*]. Now it has been suggested that the humanists were in fact borrowing from medieval publicists, who adopted this new periodisation of life, death and rebirth in order to attack the papacy's imperial pretensions: what was new about this scheme in the Renaissance was its transference from church history 'to secular culture and history' [34 *esp. p. 66*].

But instead of dismissing the idea of rebirth because it was derivative or a legend, we should perhaps see it as an attempt at a new beginning that disguised its newness by claiming to have cultural links with the ancient past. Like the French revolutionaries who rewrote their past in this way in 1789, as De Certeau describes [in 38 p. 13], Renaissance people may have been engaged on a similar enterprise, that is, re-writing and updating their past by deciding what to discard as 'dead' and what to retain as a crucial link with their earlier history. The fact that the language of rebirth was associated with progress and freedom suggests it too had a political purpose, that of legitimising the self-governing communes in northern Italy. For it was humanists in Padua – then succumbing to despotic government – who first suggested that political freedom was essential for a thriving culture, to be followed by Coluccio Salutati and Leonardo Bruni in Florence, which was also

fighting to preserve its independence [134 *p. 165; Doc. 3*]. By the sixteenth century the same idea was applied by Vasari in his *Lives of the
Artists* to account for the decline of architecture and painting from
the time of the Roman emperors to their gradual revival with the rebirth of the early communes, 'to reach perfection in our own times' in
the art of Michelangelo and Titian [*Doc. 4*].

Although the idea of rebirth was well established in Italy by the
sixteenth century, it was not until the eighteenth and nineteenth
centuries that the term 'Renaissance' was used to describe a separate
historical period with its own underlying coherence. Surprisingly,
perhaps, we first meet the Renaissance in its familiar juxtaposition
with the Middle Ages not in a history, but in a novel by Balzac of
1829, in which he says of one of the leading characters: 'She could
argue fluently on Italian or Flemish painting, on the Middle Ages or
the Renaissance', suggesting that it was already a familiar concept by
then. So the French historian Jules Michelet (1798–1874) was not,
strictly speaking, 'the inventor' of the Renaissance, as he has been
called; but he was the first person to write a book about the Renaissance (in 1855) and to invent the phrases 'the discovery of the world'
and 'the discovery of man' to describe it. It was these concepts that
Burckhardt used in his *Civilisation of the Renaissance* [44] and which
have been recently under attack, for the reasons described in the
Introduction. His dependence on the Italian humanists raises the
question of how far they in turn were dependent on the language and
ideas of earlier revivals.

3 EARLIER RENAISSANCES, 800–1300

Classical culture had never entirely disappeared from Europe, thanks to the protection afforded to ancient manuscripts by monastery libraries after the division and disintegration of the Roman empire in the fifth century AD. After Charlemagne was crowned in Rome on Christmas Day 800, however, he attempted to restore the Roman empire in the west by stimulating a widespread revival of Roman literature, art and architecture, as well as of political institutions. This is what is called the first important classical 'renewal' or *renovatio* in the eighth and ninth centuries. Classical texts were studied critically and collated by scholars like Lupus of Ferrières. They were then copied in manuscripts that were decorated with illustrations modelled on classical drawings and written in a clear, round hand that fifteenth-century humanists later imitated, thinking it was ancient – thanks to whom the printed type we now read today is in fact Carolingian in origin rather than genuinely classical. Literary biographies such as Einhard's *Life of Charlemagne* were written on the model of Suetonius's *Lives of the Emperors* and in new palace schools the classical curriculum was taught again by scholars like Alcuin, whom Charlemagne brought from York to instruct his household. Alcuin hoped to combine 'Plato's academy in the seven liberal arts' with 'the teachings of our Lord Jesus Christ' to create a new Athens in the imperial court [122 *p. 15*]. There was an architectural revival, too, with Vitruvius's *Treatise on Architecture*, as well as surviving Roman buildings, providing the model for Charlemagne's palace at Aachen. The revival was widespread, and although it was followed by another period of devastation and political disorder, it did serve to keep alive classical models that might otherwise have disappeared during continuing barbarian invasions.

The next important revival in the twelfth century is regarded by some historians as more important than the fifteenth-century Renaissance, in that it was more widely diffused and resulted in the great systematisation of scientific knowledge and logic called 'scholasticism' that dominated European universities until at least the seventeenth century [32 *p. 71*]. It also came at a time of great economic resurgence throughout Europe: as a result of the Crusades and expanding frontiers, trade increased and towns developed everywhere, especially in Italy. In fact, this second revival Philip Jones would prefer to call a 'revolution' rather than a rebirth, since its market values and proto-capitalism were 'a negation of antiquity' – unlike the later 'Italian Renaissance', which did see a revival of the civic and aristocratic values of classical antiquity [94 *pp. 4–5, 50–54*].

The growth of urban centres in southern France and Italy encouraged a demand for more participation in politics and a more secular culture for the many scribes, notaries and officials who administered these towns. Roman law and history were particularly relevant to them, as they were to the administrators of the increasingly independent monarchies that were emerging in northern Europe. Although these administrators were usually clerics in religious orders, the chancellors of royal and episcopal curias – such as John of Salisbury (d. 1180) and Peter of Blois (c. 1120–1200) – were as enthusiastic about classical culture as their urban and secular counterparts in self-governing communes. Thanks to them, cathedrals as well as palaces were decorated in the new 'Romanesque' style: classical images of the Seven Liberal Arts combined with worshipping angels to adorn the west door of Chartres cathedral in the middle of the twelfth century. The framework remained Christian but within it emphasis gradually shifted from the supernatural to man. For this reason Richard Southern calls the period from 1100 to 1320 'one of the great ages of humanism in the history of Europe: perhaps the greatest of all' [144 *p. 31*].

The new element in the twelfth-century intellectual revival that made it different from earlier and later ones was a re-awakened interest in Greek science and philosophy. This was stimulated by renewed contact with the East through the crusades, and with Arab Spain. These subjects had largely disappeared from the West, but they had survived in the East in Arab translations and commentaries, such as in the *Almagest*, an Arab version of the astronomical system of Ptolemy (a Greek scientist who lived in the second century AD), or in the commentaries of Avicenna (980–1037) and Averroes (1126–98) on Aristotle. Now scholars from the West like Gerard of Cremona (1114–87) and Michael Scot (before 1200–*c*. 1235) went to Toledo to learn Arabic in order to study and translate these writings, as well as Euclid's *Elements* and Archimedes' scientific treatises. Thanks to them, a vast new body of scientific knowledge that had been lost to the West for centuries was suddenly made available to scholars throughout Europe.

Its impact was immense. Aristotle had written about metaphysics, physics, meteorology, astronomy and biology, as well as about logic, politics and ethics, and most of these scientific works were now translated into Latin for the first time. Among the results was the re-emergence of new 'licensed' teachers who formed 'universities' (or guilds). Yet it is a measure of the threat this material posed to Christian culture that very soon students in the new university of Paris were prohibited from reading Aristotle. For whereas the Latin classics had been assimilated by being allegorised – Ovid's portrait of the Greek god Ganimede, for instance, was interpreted as a prefiguration of John the Baptist instead of as a beautiful youth whom Plato thought justified men's love for boys – the new scientific writings directly threatened Christian doctrine about the structure of the world and the role of God. According to Aristotle, once the world had been set in motion, it was governed by eternal rational laws in which there was no further role for the Prime Mover, or God. Moreover, Aristotle did not believe in individual immortality or the resurrection of the body. As for inherited sin, he thought that man, far from being sinful, was naturally sociable and capable of governing himself in political communities.

These ideas, if accepted, would have undermined the whole structure of the Christian world with its belief in God's power and providential grace administered through the Church. In 1210 the new natural philosophy was banned in the university of Paris, in 1215 the ban was extended, and in 1277 a list was compiled of 219 condemned 'errors'. The breach between Greek determinism and Christian providence seemed irreconcilable. However, instead of bringing the revival to an abrupt halt, something different happened. Greek philosophy and science were christianised by two Dominican friars, St Albert the Great (*c.* 1220–80) and St Thomas Aquinas (*c.* 1226–74). The crisis had been resolved – at any rate on the surface – by imposing a Christian interpretation on classical science as well as on classical literature. For this reason the art historian Erwin Panofsky [121] argues that the twelfth- and thirteenth-century revival was not a true revival of classicism because there was, as he puts it, 'disjunction' between the content, or meaning, and the form, or outward expression, of classical images. So we find Cicero dressed as a monk while Eve is modelled on a pagan Cupid – without the artists feeling any sense of anachronism.

In fact it proved difficult to reconcile classical ideas with Christian ones, especially in the field of science where Greek determinism conflicted with Christian free will. In the fourteenth century a new reform movement developed that attacked the scientists and university men who admired Aristotle for being 'moderns' in contrast to the 'ancients', meaning by 'ancients' not genuine classical writers but rather twelfth-century humanists. This was the movement headed by Petrarch, with whom the history of the Italian Renaissance must still begin.

4 ITALIAN COMMUNES AND CITY-STATES, *c.* 1300

Most of Europe around 1300 was governed by kings assisted by a restricted ruling class of ecclesiastics and nobles, the first and second estates of medieval society. These were the men who controlled cities and towns, rather than the traders and artisans who lived and did business in them. Italy and southern France were different. There cities had survived from the Roman period which were still centres of urban life and culture; and although churchmen and nobles were a dominant force in these cities as elsewhere, the townspeople had begun to insist on having a share of government from the eleventh century onwards – and in some cities they even took over the government, calling themselves 'communes' when they had ousted the churchmen and nobles from their monopoly of power.

Italy had more of these self-proclaimed communes than other countries, partly because city life had never died out in the Mediterranean south, even during the worst of the barbarian invasions, and partly because trade revived earlier in Italy than elsewhere. Because their overlords were German emperors who only came to Italy intermittently – to gather taxes and to be crowned in Milan and then Rome – Italian cities, especially in Lombardy and Tuscany, had early on begun to feel independent and enjoy limited self-government. The German chronicler Otto of Freising commented on this when he visited Italy in the twelfth century. 'Almost the whole territory is divided into cities', he wrote, which were governed by annually-elected consuls drawn from the 'plebs' or common people as well as from the knightly class: 'nor is there scarcely a noble or great man who does not obey the city government'. Otto, like another visitor, the Jewish chronicler Benjamin Tudela, was clearly impressed by the freedom and independence of the Italians, since, as Tudela put it, they 'possess neither king nor prince to govern them but only the judges appointed by themselves'. In saying that their government and love of liberty were modelled on Ancient Roman republicanism ('in which they imitate the intelligence of ancient Romans'), Otto already draws our attention to what were to become the two associated themes of Renaissance rhetoric, republicanism and liberty [154].

Now we are more sceptical about the extent of the independence and freedom of Italian cities and of the role of 'plebs' and artisans in their governments. According to Philip Jones [94 *pp. 588–600*], in 'big business' Florence the major offices were monopolised by a few super-rich guildsmen – merchants, bankers, lawyers and later wool-drapers – who were closer in outlook to the nobility than to ordinary members of the populace. Apart from a few 'radical interludes', as Jones calls them, the policies of these communes remained conservative and restrictive, their outlook upper-class, not populist.

Nevertheless, the argument stressing the continuity of aristocratic power in Italy is not unchallenged. According to John Najemy [114], the people – that is, tradespeople, artisans and workers – kept the republican argument alive, even if they were only intermittently powerful, and they prevented the nobility and oligarchs from exercising an absolute monopoly of power. It was the existence of so many merchants, traders and artisans that made the culture of Italian cities distinctive. And it was these men, not the nobles, Richard Goldthwaite argues, who created the consumer boom that stimulated the artistic revival; for they made and paid for the art and artefacts that adorned the new Renaissance palaces and chapels, stimulating not only the building trade but also innumerable other artisan skills and products [76 *pp. 33–62*].

The wealth of Italian cities also derived from trade with the rest of Europe and the East, and this too contributed to the distinctive ethos of city life in Italy. It was the merchant-chronicler Gregorio Dati who wrote, 'whoever is not a merchant and hasn't investigated the world and seen foreign nations and returned with possessions to his native home is considered nothing' [*Doc. 7*]. And when the king of Portugal's conquest of Guinea was read out in the square in Florence in 1486, it was regarded in the city as 'splendid and great news', not simply for the merchandise and profit involved but because the natives would be introduced 'to a human and not a bestial life'. So trade and conquest were not only enriching but also 'civilising' in the eyes of contemporaries.

There are other reasons apart from wealth, however, that help to explain why this revival took the form it did in Italy, to do with its classical inheritance. Classical culture was still thriving in Italian cities, which based their statutes on Roman law and practised classical rhetoric in their law-courts and council-chambers. Far from being 'dead' authors, Cicero, Virgil and other Roman writers were taught to children in city schools as preparation for the active civic life that awaited them. Classical history, too, was seen to be relevant to these burgeoning cities as they competed with each other to claim more ancient and illustrious ancestors. In Padua, for example, a local notary and one of the earliest humanists in Italy, Lovato Lovati (1241–1309), erected a monument to the city's alleged founder, the Trojan Antenor. In the next generation his pupil Albertino Mussato (1261–1329) was the first poet to be crowned with a laurel-wreath, like the Romans, and he was also one of the first humanists to write a patriotic history and a play about his city, the *Historia Augusta* and *Ecerinis*, in which he used the Roman writers Livy and Seneca as a source of political advice.

Similarly in Florence, the humanist Brunetto Latini (*c.* 1220–94?) used his classical learning to praise his city. In addition to being a teacher and writing a small encyclopedia of knowledge, *The Treasure*, Latini was chancellor of the first 'popular' government of the city from 1250 to 1260. As chancellor, he inscribed the government's new palace (now the National Museum) with jingoistic lines that reveal his civic pride in Florence: 'She rules the land, she rules the sea, she rules the whole territory. Thus by her domination all Tuscany becomes prosperous, just as Rome continues to triumph by coercing everyone under her declared law.'

Brunetto Latini's reference to Rome shows the importance of Rome as a model for the new communes – but a model of what? Initially it seemed clear that it was a model of freedom and self-government. The earliest officials of the Italian communes had been called 'consuls' like their Roman forebears, and their councils also resembled those of republican Rome: both had an aristocratic senate, or Council of the Commune, and a popular Tribunate, or Council of the People, together forming the SPQR, the 'Senatus Populusque Romanus' (or as the Florentines translated it, the SPQF, Senatus Populusque Florentinus). But Latini's verse reminds us that republican Rome was also the centre of a world empire, which it dominated by force of arms and law – the 'Roman law' that Latini referred to. Both aspects of Rome must have appealed to Italian cities as they expanded into 'city-states' with subject populations under their control. Later the historian Francesco Guicciardini was to write that no one wants to be born a subject, but it was worse to be the subject of a republic than of a prince [18 *p. 173;* 19 *p. 68*] – reminding us that republicanism has two faces, an imperialist face as well as a freedom-loving one.

There were other characteristics that Italian cities shared with ancient cities. They were roughly the same size, with populations ranging from 25,000 to 100,000, and they experienced the same joys and agonies of city life. Renaissance Romans – like visitors there today – would have appreciated Juvenal's satirical account of life in Ancient Rome, where the sound of traffic made sleep impossible at night and painted, scheming women stalked the streets in search of victims. But they would also have appreciated the civility of city life: its paved streets, squares, fountains and theatres, as well as its council chambers and meeting places. It was Brunetto Latini who advised people that it was not 'urbane to move without restraint' in cities, since city-dwellers should move 'in a stately manner' and not 'squirm like eels' as though they came from the countryside [119 *p. 10*]. For as a Florentine merchant later told his sons, in the words of a familiar proverb, 'Honour does not dwell in woods; worthy men are made in cities'. By the same token men who lived in the countryside were 'barbarians' – 'beastly men who followed their nature and conversed with beasts'.

The idea that men could not be fully human or civilised unless they lived in a *civitas* and engaged in the political life of the *polis* is also a classical idea (these are the Roman and Greek words for city-state from which our adjectives 'civilised' and 'political' derive). Perhaps the Italians always shared it too. But we know that they did after the middle of the thirteenth century when Aristotle's famous book, *The Politics*, was translated into Latin. For the Dominican teacher and preacher, fra Remigio Girolami [d. 1319], then quoted Aristotle's opinion that 'he who is not a citizen is not a man', illustrating this in his own striking image of a citizen whose city is destroyed remaining 'a painted image or a form of stone, because he will lack the virtue and activity of former times'. This seems a surprising view for a Dominican friar, for whom the demands of the state should never take precedence over the salvation of individual souls, but as an Italian and a member of a prominent political family, Remigio evidently agreed with Aristotle that it was wrong for anyone to think he belonged just to himself: his affairs were the concern of the city as a whole.

Closely related to this idea was the sense of patriotism or *campanilismo*, as Italians still call their love for the *campanile* or bell-tower of their own birth-place. This love provided a great incentive for embellishing one's town with art and architecture, for as one preacher said, beauty is part of the 'order' of a city that contributes to its civilising effect, as it had done in classical times. Concepts of urban planning developed early in Italian towns, as we can see from government decrees that speak of 'beauty' and 'utility' as twin ideals. Spurred on by patriotic rivalry, communes and lordships competed for the beauty prize. Florence hoped to have 'a more beautiful and honourable temple than any other existing in Tuscany' in 1300; Siena in 1316 wanted her officials to 'occupy beautiful and honourable dwellings, both for the sake of the commune and because foreigners often visit their houses on affairs'; and Azzo Visconti, Lord of Milan, desired to construct a magnificent palace for himself after making peace with the pope, for (quoting from Aristotle's *Ethics*) 'it is the work of a magnificent man to erect a fine dwelling, for people who see marvellous buildings are deeply impressed with strong admiration' [*105 p. 101*].

Day-to-day life in Italian cities in the thirteenth century was of course very different from the classical ideal. Far from being 'civilised', cities were distinguished by the violence and disorder created by a feuding nobility, a rich and restless merchant class and a rootless proletariat. Since the feudal consular class and the Church remained powerful forces in cities, we should not exaggerate the republicanism and democracy of the cities either. Many were already falling into the hands of single lords or *signori* who rapidly brought the communal era to an end and, as we have seen, republicanism was more an ideal rather than a reality – though none the less powerful for that.

Historians rightly stress the importance of royal and ecclesiastical courts as the wealthiest and most influential patrons in the late medieval period. In Italy the cultural pattern was different. For instead of enjoying a single centre of patronage comparable with the great courts of kings and emperors elsewhere, Italy enjoyed a web of interconnected and competitive cities with links to the East and northern Europe. Together they formed clusters of talent that gravitated like constellations around larger and richer cities – such as Florence, Siena and Padua – as well as the Papal court in Rome and the court of the kings of Naples. Thus the artist and architect Giotto (1267?–1337) worked in Rome and Naples as well as in Florence and Padua, while the sculptor Nicola Pisano (*c.* 1220–*c.* 1284) and his son Giovanni (*c.* 1245–after 1314), also worked in the south as well as in Pisa, Siena and Padua. So Italy offered fertile soil for an early renaissance. It was wealthy. Its cities were competitive. And it enjoyed a sense of affinity with ancient ideas of civility, beauty and magnificence that made this revival different from the twelfth-century revival.

5 THE RISE OF LORDSHIPS AND THE BLACK DEATH

Stable though this environment seemed, a series of political and economic crises – foreign invasions, economic recession and the devastating plague of 1348 that nearly halved Italy's population – seemed to threaten cultural development in the fourteenth century. According to one contemporary, art since Giotto's day 'has grown and continues to grow worse day by day' [111 *p. 3*] and in some cities building projects were halted or slowed down – the cathedral in Siena still today remaining in a half-finished state. Moreover, most of the centres of the cultural revival – the independent cities described in the previous chapter – fell into the hands of single rulers or lords, threatening the civic programmes of the earlier communes.

These developments in turn seemed to challenge earlier assumptions about the Renaissance, giving rise in the 1960s to a debate between Robert Lopez and Richard Goldthwaite about the cultural revival: did it develop from an economic recession, as Lopez argued [108], or from economic growth, as Goldthwaite instead proposed [76 *p. 14 and* n. 2]? The debate has now been reassessed by Judith Brown, who argues that although there was an overall decline in trade and trade-generated wealth in the course of the fourteenth and early-fifteenth centuries, due to the population decrease, this seems to have resulted in diversification and the growth of new wealth among survivors rather than a sustained depression [39]. There is certainly no evidence to support Lopez's argument that people responded by 'investing in culture' – as though they were present-day brokers and investors buying art to store in bank-safes – since there was as yet no established art-market and no concept of art as a sound investment, although both did develop by the end of the period.

More convincing is Richard Goldthwaite's argument that Italy at this time offered 'the preconditions for luxury consumption'. The Black Death left its survivors richer than before, both from inherited wealth and from increased wages. New silk and cotton industries were developing, and the trade that had been lost to northern Europe – thanks to the Hundred Years War and the Schism – was more than made up for by trade in the Mediterranean, especially with Spain and with the Ottoman court at Constantinople after its fall to the Turks in 1453, this benefited not only Venice and Genoa but also Florence, a new competitor for trade in the east after conquering Pisa in 1406 and building its own maritime fleet.

The Black Death and its aftermath encouraged consumption in other ways. By leaving its survivors much richer than before and keen to rise in the world, it acted as a direct incentive to spending and luxurious living. As Samuel Cohn's study of wills has demonstrated, it also encouraged people to leave memorials of themselves in chapels, tombs and paintings. Nor was it only rich nobles and their wives who wanted to memorialise themselves with coats-of-arms and portraits: a blacksmith's son wanted to be depicted with his father in a sacred painting, labelled 'Here is Montagne the Blacksmith, here is Pasquino [his son]', and so too did a notary's widow, to preserve 'her true memory' [*55 pp. 111, 225*].

It is not easy to distinguish religious motivation – the desire for salvation in the face of sudden death – from social motivation or 'the new-rich factor'. Even before the Black Death, outlay on chapels and chantries had been encouraged by the Mendicants, who preached the possibility of salvation in Purgatory through masses and the charitable endowments of their survivors; and afterwards growing fear of sudden death served to increase 'liturgical apparatus', expenditure on chapels and on masses for the dead [*76 pp. 72–6*].

At the same time, the plague increased social mobility at all levels of society. In republics like Florence, where there was no closed political elite, people were particularly keen to record their social and political status, as we shall see. Art and conspicuous consumption in the form of houses, possessions and clothes, were all ways of demonstrating status and contributing to a cultural revival. But the new-rich factor applies as much to courts as to city-states, since the lords who had seized power were often new men themselves, as former *condottieri* or mercenary soldiers, and as new rulers they certainly needed all the help that art and artefacts could give them to establish their authority – statues, triumphal arches, chapels, medals and portraits. Few dared to go as far as Bernabo Visconti, who placed a gilded figure of himself on the campanile of Milan cathedral in the 1330s [*157 pp. 231–2*], but they all used art to glory themselves and their courts.

Recent emphasis on the importance of courts has also reopened the debate about whether political independence was as crucial to artistic achievement as nineteenth-century writers like John Stuart Mill had thought. As Evelyn Welch has said, in a signorial dominion, the lord was the law and the prince could spend his wealth on public and private projects as he wanted, giving immediate effect to Aristotle's definition of princely magnificence. So although the only royal court, or *curia*, in Italy was that of the Angevins in Naples (especially after the papal court moved to Avignon, where it remained until the middle of the next century), there were many other newly-established princely courts which rapidly expanded to fill the cultural vacuum – until the return of the Aragonese to Naples in 1443 and the Papacy to Rome a year later drew them once more into a wider orbit. The centre of this wider orbit, it eventually became clear, was Rome, the home of the High Renaissance.

Until then, smaller constellations of talent formed around the old centres of communal power, now transformed into lordships. Padua, a centre of the early renaissance, was ruled (with interruptions) by the Carrara family after 1318, as Parma was ruled by the Correggio family. In Milan, the Visconti family, who ruled from 1329, were successful in becoming dukes in 1395, unlike the Sforza family who seized power in 1450. Ferrara's rulers, the Este family, became marquises in 1393 and dukes in 1471; in Mantua, the Gonzaga family were created marquises in 1433 and dukes in 1530; and in Urbino, the Montefeltro were created dukes in 1443. The rulers of the leading courts were thus all newly ennobled by the emperor (or the pope). They were also newly rich, since as paid professional soldiers or *condottieri*, they were wealthy and could afford grandiose artistic enterprises to reinforce their status.

For these reasons 'the disastrous fourteenth century' now challenges some of our earlier preconceptions about the origins of the fifteenth-century revival. Far from being a set-back, the fourteenth century now appears to have contributed more to the Renaissance than we once thought – not least, the figure of Petrarch, who from many points of view must still be regarded as founder of the Renaissance movement. Although claimed by Florence as one of the three 'outstanding men whom our city has borne in these times', Petrarch's special achievement as a poet and writer owes little to Florence and much more to the crises of this period – exile in France, the Black Death, and his subsequent peripatetic existence in northern Italy. So if he typifies Renaissance values, perhaps they too owe more to fourteenth-century developments than we have been led to believe.

6 THE PARADOX OF PETRARCH (1304–74)

Although an Italian by birth, Francesco Petrarca spent his formative years outside Italy, first in Carpentras, where his father went to live after being exiled from Florence, and then in Avignon. Far from disadvantaging him, however, the seventeen years Petrarch spent in the household of Bishop Giacomo and Cardinal Giovanni Colonna in Avignon opened him to a world of culture that was more stimulating – and formative – than Italy was at the time. It was there that he first acquired a knowledge of classical literature and embarked on what became a lifelong passion, his hunt for ancient manuscripts [158 p. 10]. As an exile Petrarch was also more aware than his own countrymen of the cultural heritage of Italy – 'my Italy', as he called it in a moving poem – and he was more resentful than they were of the Papacy's prolonged absence from Rome, which was still revered as the ancient centre of the Roman empire and the rightful seat of the Papacy.

After returning to Italy he was constantly on the move, first patronised by the Correggio lords of Parma, then by the Visconti lords of Milan, by Andrea Dandolo in Venice and finally by the Carrara lords of Padua, near to whom, at Arquà, he finally built himself a country house where he lived until his death in 1374. With the perception of an outsider, he first put into words many of the feelings and ideas that we now think of as characterising the Renaissance as it later developed: sensitivity to nature, an unashamed desire for glory as well as for physical love – which Petrarch described as 'two adamantine chains' from which he tried to escape but couldn't – the cultivation of friendship through letter-writing, and above all, a close rapport with classical literature.

It was Petrarch's experience of the Black Death, however, that may have inspired his most famous writing, the *Canzoniere*. According to a recent account of his poetry-writing, Petrarch found in classical literature 'a channel' through which to express and withstand his ancestral fears of death – fears triggered by the devastating plague of 1348–50, which killed his beloved Laura [*Doc. 6*] and many of his friends. By turning his scattered thoughts about himself and his life into a book of verse, the *Canzoniere*, he created for himself his own monument, or 'mausoleum', through which to withstand the assaults of time [136 *p. 10*]. This process of self-construction to acquire immortality seems very modern, but it was Petrarch's classical sensibility that encouraged him to react towards the prospect of annihilation in this way – and this remains one of the enduring and important features of the Renaissance we are investigating.

Letter-writing, too, contributed to his self-construction, since Petrarch, like Cicero, published his 'familiar letters' as part of his attempt to unify fragmented episodes of his life into a collective whole. So too did art. It can be no coincidence that more painted portraits survive of Petrarch than of any of his contemporaries. Though not a painter himself, Petrarch patronised new painters like Simone Martini [*c.* 1284–1344], who painted a portrait of Laura, as well as a cover for Petrarch's equally beloved copy of Virgil, both important figures in his life-story. He also patronised Giotto, by whom he owned a painted Madonna. Fittingly, Petrarch himself is immortalised in the Hall of the Famous Men in Padua together with the famous ancients he had immortalised in *De viris illustribus*.

Despite the seeming paradox of his position as a man without a stable base or a patronage network in Italy, he was novel in using letters and his constant travels to sustain a coterie of friends and disciples – anticipating the extended readership, or 'republic of letters' as it has been called [65 *ch.* 4], later created by the printing press. Through them, he transformed interest in classical antiquity into a movement with common aims and prejudices, which we will investigate in Part Three: that is, a passion for books, libraries, textual criticism, invectives and 'the clear splendour of the ancient past'; a hatred of barbarism, scholasticism and obscurantist darkness. When he died in 1374, he was a famous man. He had visited Emperor Charles IV in Prague, who created him a Count Palatine, the King of France in Paris, and the popes in Avignon. He refused all their invitations to remain at their courts, 'in order,' he said, 'to retain my liberty'. He had been created Poet Laureate in Rome and was sought-after wherever he went in Italy.

Because he wrote so much and so openly about himself, Petrarch has come to typify the individualism and the 'modern' outlook of the Renaissance. Yet, as we have seen, this was largely a self-constructed portrait, so if he typifies modernity it is largely because of his success in portraying himself in this way. And the classical sensibility that gave him new insight into the past also encouraged imitation. Even his moving poem describing his ambivalent desire for love and glory – 'For when I think of glorious and generous fame I know not whether I freeze or burn, or whether I be pale or gaunt' – is copied from Catullus, making us wonder how authentic and personal these emotions were.

Yet it is Petrarch's self-awareness and self-promotion that represent his importance for the Renaissance. The extent of his influence can be seen by comparing him with Pietro Aretino, another freelance writer who lived in Italy some three hundred years later, at the height of the High Renaissance period. Unlike Petrarch, Aretino was a satirist and pornographer, not a moralist. But he too enjoyed an international reputation and, like Petrarch, he prided himself on his independence while inspiring 'awe and terror' in kings and emperors. He also disseminated his image by written and visual media – a portrait by Titian and medals which circulated in Italy and across the courts of Europe. Petrarch would not have described his own 'pen as plague-ridden ... my ink as poison and my paper as a grave', as Aretino did [161 *p. 293*], but both men used their pens to create themselves for their courtly patrons, as well as for a wider literary audience within a new republic of letters.

7 'BIG-BUSINESS' FLORENCE

Because Petrarch lacked a stable base in Italy, any one of a number of cities could have become the centre of the cultural movement he had instigated. There were groups of humanists working in close rapport in several cities – Venice, Padua, Milan and Florence – all of which were also producing impressive works of art at the time. Improbably, perhaps, it was 'big-business' Florence – or 'commercial and cloth-making' Florence, as Petrarch more disparagingly called the city (*Epist.fam.* 18.9.2) – which became the centre of a dynamic explosion of talent around 1400. Although Florence had been called 'the home of gold' by Pope Boniface VIII and had enjoyed the same civic revival as other Italian communes around 1300, its ruling merchant elite did not favour the new humanistic values promoted by Petrarch. One merchant reacted angrily when his son said he wanted to study letters instead of following his father into business; and another reacted with equal hostility to the avant-garde ideas that were being 'shouted out' in Florence's main square at the beginning of the fifteenth century [*Doc. 8*].

The reasons why the movement focused on Florence before spreading throughout Europe need investigating, since they help to explain an important difference between earlier revivals and this one. Whereas earlier civic programmes of renewal had been largely independent of scholarly revivals of classical texts, in Florence the two recovery programmes were integrated into a joint programme in which professionals, artisans and merchants all participated. Subsequently, the same types of townspeople elsewhere in Europe combined to introduce similar programmes – especially humanist tutors and grammar schools for their children, like St Paul's School in London, which still teaches the Renaissance liberal-arts curriculum today.

That this happened in Florence around 1400 is due to a combination of circumstances, some a matter of chance or luck, others to do with Florence's social and political structures. Florence was lucky to have an outstanding classical scholar as chancellor at a critical moment in its history. Coluccio Salutati (1331–1406) was the owner of the largest library of ancient manuscripts in Italy after Petrarch's death in 1374, and after his appointment at the head of Florence's administration a year later, he attracted to the city a new cluster of talent. It was thanks to him that the first Chair of Greek anywhere in Europe was established there in 1396. Although its first holder, the Greek scholar and diplomat from Constantinople, Manuel Chrysoloras (1350–1415), taught for less than three years (he then moved briefly to Padua, where he taught Greek to other students like Guarino Guarini, 1374–1460), the Chair remained, serving as a magnet in drawing to Florence a group of young men whom George Holmes has called the avant-garde of the precarious Renaissance movement [90]. Although their ideas may not seem revolutionary today, they challenged the traditional values of their fathers and teachers and mocked their religion, 'secretly preferring' the pagan Varro to the Church Fathers and attacking 'our' saints [*Doc. 8*].

It was also fortuitous that the batch of Greek books Chrysoloras acquired from Greece to teach his pupils included Ptolemy's *Geography* – a book that had a dynamic impact, as we shall see, for it not only taught perspective to Florentine artists but it contributed to the discovery of the New World [64 *pp. 93–4*]. But its impact was also due to the environment in which it arrived. For instead of being restricted to university or monastic circles, Chrysoloras's classes were open to a cross-section of Florence's new intelligentsia: mathematicians, artists, merchants, theologians and humanist administrators. They included the mathematician and astrologer Paolo Toscanelli (1397–1482); practical engineers like Filippo Brunelleschi (1377–1446); rich businessmen like Palla Strozzi (1372–1462) and Cosimo de' Medici (1389–1464), as well as the eccentric and difficult Niccolò Niccoli (1364–1437); monks like Luigi Marsili (d.1394) and Ambrogio Traversari (1386–1439), who acted as the movement's spiritual advisers; and notaries and administrators from the provinces like Coluccio Salutati (1331–1405) and Leonardo Bruni (1374–1444).

So the social and political lifestyle of Florence also played an important part in the take-off of the Renaissance movement. Its open squares or piazzas were places where people met to exchange news and gossip, especially the government square (piazza della Signoria), where political assemblies and plebiscites were held, and where people regularly encountered each other on the way to the government palace or to the Merchants' guild. It was there, under the projecting 'Roof of the Pisans', that the avant-garde gathered to shout out their provoking views. The chattering classes also met inside the shops of scribes and booksellers like Vespasiano da Bisticci, who has recorded some of his clients' gossip in a remarkable book of his own [28]. Or they met in the cathedral itself, which, as Leon Battista Alberti (1404–72) said, was 'warm in winter and cool in summer'. So in Florence, the new 'republic of letters' did not depend on the circulation of ideas through print or reputation: the city's open streets, piazzas, shops and churches – as well as its open government – all served as channels through which to diffuse the new ideas.

According to one historian, Hans Baron, writing in the 1950s, it was the political crisis of 1402 that brought all these ingredients together and transformed the avant-garde's rhetoric into heart-felt belief in the virtues of republicanism [30]. In fact, Florence was only saved from the duke of Milan's onslaught by his sudden death, but it was widely believed that Salutati's well-publicised letters against him were worth at least a thousand horses in propaganda value – and this, Baron argued, helped to bring Ancient Roman republicanism to life again as a burning political issue. This thesis has been attacked from many directions: that Florentine republicanism pre-dated 1402, that it was in any case rhetorical, since Florence's government was far more restricted and elitist than Salutati's letters suggested, and that Baron was himself too biased by his own experience of the propaganda of the Second World War.

Without relying as heavily as Baron did on the events of one year, 1402, it nevertheless remains true that republican ideology did become more widely diffused among Florentines after the early 1400s – and since it still retains the power to inspire and incite freedom movements even today, who are we to dispute its force in the fifteenth century? For the reasons we discussed in chapter 4, republicanism remained a lively issue, despite – or because of – the elitism of its government. The fact that office-holding was still restricted to members of guilds (thereby excluding the nobility) had cultural as well as political implications. The guilds had early on acquired responsibility for the most important monuments in the city – not only the cathedral, baptistery and campanile but other institutions like the oratory and grain market at Orsanmichele and, later, the Foundling Hospital of the Innocenti. This helped to inject money into institutional building projects (like business sponsorship today), and it also encouraged popular participation in these projects by enabling guildsmen to have a say in the buildings and works of art they commissioned, in this way helping to develop artistic sensibility in people from all walks of life. The competitiveness of the guilds also acted as a spur to patronage, as we can see from the decision of the Wool Guild in 1425 to remake its tabernacle and its statue in Orsanmichele because it was being out-done by the rival Cloth and Banking Guilds [*Doc. 27*]. Because of this, the Wool Guild also commissioned the fashionable Ghiberti to make the new statue of its patron saint.

Florence's guild government had other implications. The absence of a defined ruling caste encouraged greater social mobility than in other towns, and with it, greater class- or status-consciousness, as we can see from an electoral analysis by the father of the historian Francesco Guicciardini. Writing in 1484, Piero Guicciardini distin-guished five grades of citizens: at the bottom the 'extreme ignobles' and 'the lowest workers', who became the 'newer rich' as they rose through the ranks of the 'more noble artisans' to a middle group, before becoming 'ennobled commoners' just below the top class of 'the ancient nobility'. 'And thus continuously', he comments, 'new men make the grade and in order to give them a place in the govern-ing class it is necessary to eliminate from it long-established citizens; and that is what is actually done' [133 *pp. 246–7, 368–9*].

So the new-man factor – present in all post-plague cities, as we saw – was even more marked in Florence, where it acted as a great stimulus to cultural as well as political activity. It encouraged book-collecting and the writing of family memoirs or *ricordanze*, which was a special feature of Florentine society, perhaps because of its mobility and the need to record office-holding and family honours for posterity. For the same reasons it encouraged private art patronage. One of the most advanced Renaissance paintings, Masaccio's daring new *Trinity* in Santa Maria Novella, was commissioned by a close relative of one such citizen, Lorenzo Lenzi, after his term of office as head of govern-ment in 1428. And the ambitious Giovanni Rucellai used artistic patronage to re-establish his family's political fortunes after the exile of his father-in-law; Rucellai commissioned Leon Battista Alberti (1404–72), one of the foremost Renaissance architects, to build a classicising palace for himself and his family and to re-do the façade of Santa Maria Novella in Florence, with his own name sacrilegiously (as some thought) displayed on it. We know that he was aware of the political value of palace-building from the fact that in his family mem-oirs he quoted Cicero's account of how Gnaeus Octavius was elected consul because of the beautiful palace he built on the Palatine [98 *pp. 54–5*]. From this point of view, the Medici family's role as Augustan patrons of the new Golden Age must also be seen as an attempt to increase their standing in the city [79]. In employing the famous

Florentine architect Filippo Brunelleschi and the sculptor Donatello (1386–1466) to design and decorate his family burial chapel in San Lorenzo, Cosimo de' Medici, like Giovanni Rucellai (and the Gonzaga – see chapter 13), derived glory from associating with antiquity as a patron of art and architecture.

Giovanni Rucellai reminds us that the desire for status or fame was only one of many motives underlying Renaissance patronage. In accounting for the pleasure he had derived from his patronage, his wish to commemorate himself was preceded by patriotism (the *campanilismo*, or love of one's city referred to in chapter 4), and his patriotism was in turn preceded by piety (love of God) [*Doc. 23*]. As we can see from his tomb in San Pancrazio, modelled on the Holy Sepulchre, and from his pilgrimage to Rome for the 1450 Jubilee 'to win remission for sins', he was a genuinely pious man.

The desire for salvation was a strong incentive to make pious bequests and endowments, and in Florence, as in other banking cities, it was made all the more urgent by the widespread practice of usury. Though strictly forbidden by the Church, all bankers lent money at interest. We know this practice was indirectly responsible for one of the most important commissions of the early Renaissance, Giotto's frescos in the Scrovegni chapel in Padua, which was built in 1305 by Enrico Scrovegni to expiate the sins of his father, a notorious usurer. We also know that towards the end of the century one of Francesco Guicciardini's ancestors felt it necessary to discuss the problem of his father's usury with a leading theologian, the humanist scholar Luigi Marsili, for fear that his father's body would be exhumed 'as a usurer's, by petition of the Bishop'. So we can readily believe the truth of the bookseller Vespasiano da Bisticci's story about Cosimo de' Medici's guilty conscience, which pricked him into spending – on the advice of Pope Eugenius IV – 'ten thousand florins on building' [*Doc. 25*] [*79 pp. 37–8*].

Pope Eugenius IV's presence in Florence boosted art and culture in the city in another way. Florence had enjoyed a long relationship with the Papacy as its bankers, or depositaries, a role assumed by the Medici in 1420 for most of the fifteenth century. This was why both Martin V and Eugenius IV lived in Florence in the 1420s and 1430s, before they could safely return to Rome, enriching the city with the business of the papal court – as well as with the skills of its curialists, who helped to make Florence a centre of humanist scholarship at the time. When Greek scholars like Gemistus Plethon arrived for the Council, they found a receptive environment for the platonic ideas they brought with them, encouraging Cosimo de' Medici to commission from Marsilio Ficino the translation of all Plato's works. This translation helped to give Florence its reputation, in the words of the German reformer Philip Melancthon, as 'the haven of shipwrecked letters' [24 *p. 68*].

It is precisely this 'myth of Florence' as home of the Renaissance which has been under recent attack. The myth was the result, we are told, of Vasari's biased and propagandistic history, written to please the Florentine Grand Dukes, and it was sustained by Florence's popularity with foreign visitors (like Vernon Lee, quoted in chapter 1), as well as by the fact that a lot of Florentine art happens to survive (Charles Hope in *The New York Review of Books*, 31 Oct. 1996). We examined in Part One how the myth of Florence arose from writers like Ficino and Vasari. In this chapter, we have looked at its importance in providing a fertile environment for the Renaissance. Despite the myth-making, it remains true that Florence was the place where – thanks to a combination of its environment and special events (Salutati's chancellorship, the arrival of Ptolemy's *Geography*, the papacy's sojourn there and the Council of 1439) – new ideas were seized on and developed into enthusiasms that we can recognise as a coherent outlook or 'mind-set', even if they didn't appear as such at the time. What they were is the subject of Part Three.

PART THREE: RENAISSANCE PASSIONS

8   THE PASSION FOR BOOKS

There were earlier scholars who had hunted out and copied ancient manuscripts, and earlier founders of libraries [148; 129 *ch. 3*]. But it is Petrarch who describes his love of books as 'an insatiable passion which I cannot restrain, nor would I if I could ... I cannot get enough books'. In using the word *cupiditas*, or 'lust' (one of the seven deadly sins), to describe his passion and in admitting that he would never be able to curb it – nor did he *want* to – he tells us that his love of books was a vice. It was doubly a vice, not only because it was insatiable but because the objects of his desire, books, were in themselves dangerous. Shortly before, Dante had cast all pagan writers into Hell in his great poem, *The Divine Comedy*, because they had not been baptised, 'and lived before the time of Christianity' (*Inf.* iv, 35, 37). And when Petrarch later described his father's hostility to the poems and ancient literature he had been buying instead of law-books (like Martin Luther's father, he had wanted his son to be a lawyer), he says his father burnt them as if they were 'heretical books' – rescuing only two volumes, a Virgil and a Cicero, when he saw how upset his son was.

There is nothing like censorship to whet the appetite. And since the books miraculously saved from the flames became Petrarch's favourite authors, we might also suspect that the whole episode is part of Petrarch's self-construction. So, too, perhaps, is his account of how he refused to be deterred by these obstacles; instead of giving up his illicit passion, he organised search-parties of 'competent and trustworthy men' to turn out the cupboards of monks and other scholars to see if 'anything will emerge to slake my thirst, or better, to whet it'. What is important is the outcome. For by writing about his love of books as a bodily passion or appetite that had to be satisfied, Petrarch established a new attitude to books and a new language in which to talk about them. This language provides us with an invaluable clue to Petrarch's later influence, since later book-hunters, unlike earlier ones, were all afflicted by the same hunger and thirst for books as Petrarch –

as we shall see. This is why we can talk of Petrarch as a trend-setter or founder of a 'movement', the Renaissance movement. But that the movement was more than a passing fashion is clear from its important consequences: by changing people's attitude to pagan books from hostility or suspicion to affection, it dramatically increased the number of ancient books in circulation; this stimulated the creation of princely and 'public' libraries, which in turn transformed scientific learning and attitudes to history.

Among the books Petrarch acquired for himself were Livy's *Decades*; two lost orations of Cicero, including *Pro Archia*, which he found in Liège in 1333; a manuscript of Propertius found in Paris and Cicero's *Letters to Atticus* found in Verona in 1345; more orations of Cicero sent from Florence; and others from the monastery of Montecassino with part of Varro's *De lingua latina* that Boccaccio had discovered there. By the time he died, he had collected a library of about two hundred manuscripts from all over Europe, which he offered to bequeath to Venice in return for a house in which to keep them as a public library. 'What a pity I did not think of it earlier when Andrea Dandolo was Doge', he wrote twelve years before he died, 'since he would then have had the honour of establishing a public library.' For the first time since antiquity, someone had suggested the idea of a public library, and although nothing came of the idea at the time, it remained alive to influence Petrarch's successors.

We can trace the growth of a new attitude to classical writers in Petrarch's letters. Best known is the letter he wrote to the long-dead Cicero after re-discovering his *Letters to Atticus* in 1345 [*Doc. 5*]. Criticising his new friend for plunging back into the political fray instead of enjoying a peaceful old age in retirement, Petrarch bid him 'farewell, for ever. From the world of the living ... in the 1345th year from the birth of the God whom you did not know.' So a book has brought a man to life again and made him a personal friend to talk and argue with, despite the time-gap and the religious differences that separated them.

Soon the books themselves became Petrarch's friends – or enemies, like his volume of Cicero's *Letters* propped up on the floor, 'Cicero, whom I have loved and cherished since boyhood, listen to the trick he played on me.' What happened was that Petrarch's gown caught a volume of Cicero, causing the heavy tome to fall and injure his leg: 'What's this, my Cicero? Why are you wounding me?... He didn't say a thing; but the next day when I entered the room he smote me again and jokingly I put him back in his place again, but higher up, thinking he was cross to be standing on the floor.' One book leads to another, just as one friend introduces you to another, as Petrarch wrote in another letter: 'Cicero's *Academics* made Marcus Varro my beloved friend ... I first fell in love with Terence in the *Tusculan Disputations*...' And love of books, like love of people, is increased by difficulties placed in its way, as we know from Boccaccio's experience in the ancient Benedictine monastery of Montecassino, where he climbed the staircase only to find grass growing on the windowsills and dust covering the books and bookshelves. 'Turning over the manuscripts, he found many rare and ancient works with whole sheets torn out, or with the margins ruthlessly clipped. As he left the room, he burst into tears.'

As we can see, Petrarch's passion was infectious. First Giovanni Boccaccio (1313–75) caught the bug in hunting for books in Montecassino and crying at the state he found them in. Then it was Coluccio Salutati, who became chancellor of Florence in 1375, the year after Petrarch's death. He shared Petrarch's feelings for Ovid, whom he described as 'a kind of door and teacher when my passion for this sort of study first flared up as if by divine inspiration at the end of my adolescence'. He, too, got the same shock on discovering 'the whole man' in Cicero's *Familiar Letters* from Vercelli as Petrarch got on reading his *Letters to Atticus*, which for the first time since antiquity now rejoined the *Familiar Letters*, placed side by side on Salutati's shelves.

Salutati had been trying to procure copies of Petrarch's Catullus and Propertius during Petrarch's lifetime and on his death he was early in the field to acquire books from Petrarch's library. As chancellor, Salutati was unable to leave Florence to hunt for manuscripts as Petrarch had done. He was, if you like, a sedentary book collector who acted through friends and agents to build up his library of well over six hundred books – all of which he freely lent to his friends to read and copy. Like Petrarch's library, it was broken up on his death, but during his lifetime it served the function he thought a public library should serve: helping textual criticism by offering scholars all available versions of texts from which to prepare emended versions, as had been the custom in antiquity.

Growing familiarity with classical authors in turn encouraged a new critical approach to the study of ancient manuscripts. It was Petrarch again who led the way. In a fascinating reconstruction, the scholar Giovanni Billanovich has demonstrated how Petrarch put together a new manuscript of Livy's great history of Rome (now in the British Library, Harleian manuscript 2493) by re-uniting the first, third and fourth *Decades* which had previously survived quite separately, emending mistakes as he did so on the basis of comparison with other versions and his growing knowledge of ancient history [33]. His manuscript was later acquired by the famous humanist scholar Lorenzo Valla (1407–57), who added his own emendations and criticisms to form a text that – thanks to the invention of printing at this time – was never again corrupted by scribal errors (and even printing owed something to Petrarch, since it is largely thanks to his admiration for what he called 'ancient', or twelfth-century, lettering, due to his failing eyesight, that we use round or 'Roman' printing type, rather than German 'gothic', today).

Petrarch's critical approach to the study of ancient manuscripts was adopted by other scholars, including Coluccio Salutati, who used his wide knowledge of the books in his library to make new attributions, such as identifying Julius Caesar, not Julius Celsus, as the author of the *Commentaries*. He did serious research into the historical origins of Florence. Until then, it was believed that Florence had been founded at the time of Julius Caesar, but now Salutati suggested on the basis of his research that it had in fact been founded at the time of the republican Sulla – an opinion that was not modified until the humanist scholar Angelo Poliziano found evidence in another manuscript that it had been founded at a slightly later date. Salutati also used Cicero's *Letters* to re-evaluate Caesar's political role in destroying the Roman republic: 'having been head of the world, (Rome) was pushed from popular liberty into the servitude of monarchy.'

Perhaps the most far-reaching result of these studies was the appointment of someone to teach Greek in Florence. It is difficult for us to imagine a time when Homer's *Iliad* and *Odyssey* could not be read because no one could understand Greek; but when Petrarch was given a manuscript of Homer in 1348, he was unable to read it: 'Your Homer is dumb with me or rather I am deaf to him,' he wrote on receiving it. Eventually two Greeks from Calabria in southern Italy were found to teach him Greek and translate his Homer. And although plans to create a Chair of Greek in Florence did not materialise in his lifetime, they did lead to the appointment of Manuel Chrysoloras from Constantinople to teach in the university twenty years later, as we have seen.

Even before Chrysoloras arrived, Salutati had written to urge one of his students in Constantinople to bring large supplies of Greek books with him when he returned to Italy – histories, poetry, mythology, works on metrics, dictionaries, and especially the whole of Plato, Plutarch and Homer – 'and get him to hurry, to satisfy our expectation and hunger.' 'Passion', 'hunger', 'thirst': Salutati used the same words as Petrarch, and from him they spread to ever-widening circles.

According to the bookseller Vespasiano da Bisticci, Chrysoloras needed more material for his teaching once he was in Florence, 'because without books he could do nothing'. As a result, Plutarch's *Lives*, Plato's *Dialogues*, Aristotle's *Politics* and Ptolemy's illustrated *Geography* were brought to Florence to feed these hungry men and transform their outlook in important ways.

The reception of Ptolemy's *Geography* in Florence (discussed more fully in chapter 14) provides one example of the dynamism generated by this assorted group of scholars, merchants and mathematicians. These men were largely responsible for transforming book-hunting from the passion of a few scholars into something much more like book-collecting as we know it today, a combination of money, scholars with the know-how, entrepreneurs and amateur enthusiasts who together created and fed a book market. 'If any of Lorenzo's books come up for sale,' the papal secretary Poggio Bracciolini (1380–1459) wrote to Niccolò Niccoli from Rome in 1423, 'I think they will bring high prices. But, please, if there is anything good to be had at a reasonable price, be sure that your Poggio gets something.'

The money in this circle was provided by rich merchants or sons of merchants, like Antonio Corbinelli (d. 1425), Niccolò Niccoli and Palla Strozzi, who started collecting Greek manuscripts after attending Chrysoloras's classes – and Cosimo de' Medici. The scholars with the know-how were humanists like Leonardo Bruni, a leading translator and later chancellor of Florence; Guarino Guarini (1374–1460), who went back to Greece with Chrysoloras in 1403 and returned six years later with more than fifty Greek manuscripts; and Poggio Bracciolini, who was not in fact part of Chrysoloras's class but was educated in Salutati's circle (in old age appointed chancellor of Florence) and, as a papal secretary, he was one of the foremost book-hunters in this period. The entrepreneurs were men like Giovanni Aurispa (1374–1459), a Sicilian, who brought back as many as 238 books from Greece in 1423 to supply the growing demand, all but thirty of which were sold by the time he died in 1459. His spoils included Homer, Pindar, Aristophanes, Demosthenes, the whole of Plato, and many others, not to mention the tenth-century manuscript he sent Niccoli from Constantinople containing plays of Sophocles and Aeschylus, as well as Apollonius of Rhodes's *Argonautica*.

Amateur enthusiasm (as well as money) was provided by merchants like Bartolomeo Bardi, who was 'hemmed in by a host of business responsibilities and with little time to read or buy' but who wanted a few volumes that would be 'useful and pleasant'. Poggio, writing from Rome, told Niccoli to get hold of 'Suetonius, Terence and Curtius. ...

Add anything that seems good to you, for Bartolomeo is rich and wants books ... let the prices be what seems best to you.' And there was the man in Rome who wanted some of Petrarch's books from Salutati's library 'and must be humoured', Poggio wrote in 1437. 'In this curia [in Rome] and in Florence too there is a great supply of books and buyers and sellers.' These were the essential ingredients for the book market that the humanists had created in Italy by the mid-fifteenth century.

Of all these men the most difficult to document, but in many ways the most important for enabling us to understand the social roots of this literary movement, is the morose, polemical and silent Niccolò Niccoli. The son of a rich cloth manufacturer in Florence whose fortune was soon dissipated after being divided between his six sons, Niccoli was a member of Chrysoloras's classes and may well have been the man who infected the artists in this group with a passion for everything classical: 'baring his arms and probing ancient buildings in order to explain the laws of architecture, diligently explaining the ruins and half-collapsed vaults of destroyed cities, how many steps there were in the ruined theatre ... how many feet the base is wide', as one humanist described him. He collected antique cameos and sculptures as well as books, impressing friends and enemies alike with his reverence for the antique: 'To see him at table like this', Vespasiano wrote in his life of Niccoli, 'looking like a figure from the ancient world, was a noble sight indeed.' The role of catalysts, Ernst Gombrich suggests [77 *p.* 72], is 'to effect a change through their mere presence, through conversation and argument ... unknown to posterity if others had not left records of their encounters', and this is what he thinks Niccoli achieved by means of his passionate and pervasive obsession with antiquity.

Above all, it is for his collection of ancient, especially Greek, manuscripts that Niccoli is famous. He was one of the first humanists to possess manuscripts of Pliny's *Natural History* and Ptolemy's *Geography*. In addition to collecting over 146 Greek manuscripts, he was an enthusiastic collector of Latin manuscripts, which he acquired with the help of his friend, Poggio Bracciolini. The correspondence of these two Renaissance book-hunters, as they have been called [11], gives a vivid picture of the excitement – and difficulties – of the hunt. In a famous letter to Guarino Guarini [*Doc. 9*], Poggio describes his heroic rescue of Quintilian's book *De institutione oratoria* from imprisonment in the monastery library of St Gall on Lake Constance, which Poggio visited while attending the council held there to end the Schism in 1414–18. Among other treasures in 'this prison house of the barbarians where they confine such men as Quintilian', Poggio also found Valerius Flaccus's *Argonauticon* and some commentaries on Cicero's *Orations* which he rapidly copied, 'so I might send them to Leonardo Bruni and Niccolò (Niccoli) in Florence: and when they heard from me of my discovery of this treasure, they urged me at great length in their letters to send them Quintilian as soon as possible.' Once rescued, Quintilian's book on how to train an orator became immensely influential in the new educational programme of humanist reformers in Italy.

A visit to the English countryside in February 1420 afforded Poggio 'no pleasure for a number of reasons ... but particularly because I found no books.' The monasteries, he explained, 'were very rich but new, having been founded since the Norman Conquest, 'so you had better give up hope of books from England, for they care very little for them here.' So the book-hunting bug had not yet spread to England, although – thanks partly to Poggio's visit – it soon did (see chapter 14). But once safely back in Italy, his passion revived: 'my thirst for books is increasing' he wrote on one occasion, and on another, 'the bug has bitten me and while the fever is on it helps and pushes me. Please send Lucretius ... the little books of Nonius Marcellus ... the *Orator* and the *Brutus* – beside I need Cicero's *Letters to Atticus*.' Stimulated by these ancient texts, Poggio began to collect what he called 'a sort of furnishing of books' for himself, for which he constructed a small building in the Tuscan countryside, where, as he told a friend, they 'might repose themselves in my absence', personifying his books just as Petrarch had done. 'I would call it a library if the paucity of books merited it.' But it was Niccoli, not Poggio, who succeeded in creating the first 'public library, to be for ever useful to men', as Poggio put it on Niccoli's death in 1439. Why was this ?

The desire for fame and immortality was doubtless important, although it was Cosimo de' Medici who eventually won more fame than Niccoli for housing his books in San Marco. Niccoli had initially left his books to Ambrogio Traversari's Camaldulensian monastery in Florence on condition that they were to be used not only by the monks but by 'all studious citizens'; but after Traversari left Florence to become general of his Order, Niccoli left the administration of his books, and the library that was to be built for them, to the discretion of his trustees. The list of these trustees shows how wide his social circle was, since it consisted of three members of the rich Medici banking family, including Cosimo; four chancery men, including Bruni and Poggio; three Florentine merchants and lawyers; the mathematician Paolo Toscanelli; and his own second cousin, plus another cousin, two more citizens and fra Ambrogio Traversari added in 1437.

This list suggests another more altruistic motive for Niccoli's public library, the desire to benefit his fellow citizens. In his *Dialogues*, Bruni attributed to Niccoli the idea that books and teachers were essential for the educational reform that Florence's abysmal cultural achievement made necessary [12; 124]; and he returned to this theme in the letter he wrote on Niccoli's death, in which he describes Niccoli as a father, in sustaining him with books as a natural father sustains his son with food. Niccoli, he wrote, wanted 'all eager for education to be able to harvest the rich fruit of learning as from a fertile field.' It was Niccoli who persuaded Piero de' Pazzi to study Greek and Latin in opposition to the intentions of his father, who 'was a merchant ... and had rather his son had been a merchant', as Vespasiano da Bisticci puts it [28 *p.310*]. So although no scholar himself, nor even a committed patriot (he was attacked for his disinterest in politics and for his disordered life-style in co-habiting with his mistress), he nevertheless seems to have shared the motivation of later businessmen like John Rylands and Walter Newberry, whose wealth was used to found public libraries in Manchester and Chicago in the nineteenth century.

Other libraries were built by popes and princes for the benefit 'of the learned', as we shall see; but the story of Niccoli's library illuminates several distinctive Renaissance themes: civic commitment to learning, as well as an individual's passion for books; a desire for the prestige and immortality that owning books, as well as writing them, bestow; and the importance of money and rich patrons. The importance of money became apparent four years after Niccoli's death in 1437, when his trustees agreed to allow Cosimo to place the books in the reformed Dominican monastery of San Marco and to exercise responsibility for them until the library was built for them there. Cosimo agreed to pay all Niccoli's debts up to the sum of 700 florins (an inexpensive way of acquiring books for San Marco) and a plaque was to be placed in the library stating that the books had belonged to Niccoli and had been preserved in great part by the generosity of Cosimo.

Cosimo de' Medici had been involved in the humanist movement for some time. He was a pupil of Roberto Rossi and had had Cicero's *Letters to Atticus* copied for him by Poggio in 1408, Livy's *Decades* soon afterwards. He had assisted Poggio's discoveries with his money and banking facilities, and in the years that followed he used both to build up his library, which by the death of his grandson Lorenzo in 1492 consisted of over one thousand books. He also commissioned the translation of Greek books – Diogenes Laertius's *Lives of the Philosophers* from Ambrogio Traversari and all of Plato's *Dialogues* and some Hermetic writings from his doctor's son, Marsilio Ficino. These books formed the basis of the Medicis' private collection of books, which was transformed during the later fifteenth century into a more grandiose library self-consciously modelled on the papal and princely libraries in Rome, Naples and Hungary. The missing gaps were filled with vast, beautifully transcribed and decorated volumes that were to be displayed publicly on the desks of the purpose-built library designed by Michelangelo, the Laurenziana, still today the Mecca of scholars from all over the world [106 *ch.4*].

The model for such a library had been provided by Cosimo's friend Tommaso Parentucelli, who conceived the idea of a public or 'Vatican' library of Greek and Latin books, as distinct from a purely papal or private one, after he became Pope Nicholas V (1447–55). Although he died before finishing this library 'for the common convenience of the learned', it was continued by Sixtus IV (1471–84), who added a fourth room to the existing Greek, Latin and private libraries, appointed librarians, and in his foundation charter of 1475 endorsed Nicholas V's programme in stating that the library was 'for the convenience and honour of the learned and studious' as well as 'for the enhancing of the church militant (and) for the increase of the Catholic faith'. It remained for a later pope, Sixtus V (1585–90) to rebuild the library and add Hebrew to the languages represented in it, following the precedent established in universities since 1499 [84 *pp. xii–xiv*].

The library that outdid either Cosimo's library or the Vatican – according to Vespasiano da Bisticci, who copied manuscripts for all of them – was that of the duke of Urbino, Federigo of Montefeltro (now the Fondo Urbinato in the Vatican library). This was because his library was not only beautifully equipped, but it alone attempted to be comprehensive in including different types of writings, in Latin, Greek and Hebrew, as well as all the works of individual authors – following the canon of texts drawn up by Nicholas V for Cosimo [28 *pp. 104–5*]. In Venice, Petrarch's plan for instituting a public library in the city was realised when Cardinal Bessarion bequeathed his books to the city in 1468, the foundation of another famous library, the Biblioteca Marciana. Salutati had dreamed of a public library where scholars could produce critical editions of texts from all available sources; a hundred years later his dream had almost come true, thanks to the combined efforts of patrons like Pope Nicholas V and the Medici – as well as scholars like Lorenzo Valla and Angelo Poliziano.

■

These scholars introduced new standards of historical and literary criticism that changed people's attitudes to the past. It was Lorenzo Valla (in his history of King Alfonso of Naples, 1445–46) who first compared the skills of a historian with those of a judge or a doctor, anticipating by more than half a century Machiavelli's better-known comparison in his *Discourses on the Decades of Livy* (I, preface) [20 *pp. 97–9*]. Valla is more famous for his exposure of the *Donation of Constantine* as a medieval forgery. He was not the first to use philology to invalidate a historical document, nor the only scholar to dispute the *Donation*: Petrarch had criticised a document for Emperor Charles IV in 1355, and the *Donation* was disputed by a German scholar as well as an English scholar at this time. They are all evidence that 'the new sense of history was growing', even though, as Peter Burke says, Valla's was 'the most elaborate and systematic criticism' and shows how closely philology and the sense of history were connected [47 *pp. 50–8*].

Even more influential were Lorenzo Valla's books of philological criticism, the *Elegantiae* and *Emendationes*, which later influenced Erasmus's work on the *New Testament* [*Doc. 11*]. But it was Angelo Poliziano who became the foremost classical scholar of the Renaissance period. His 'brilliantly original' *Miscellany* of 1489 [82 *p.22*] not only introduced new and better rules for correcting and explaining texts but did so in the form of highly readable chapters instead of in overladen and deadening commentaries. Poliziano combined his thorough knowledge of Greek sources with historical and epigraphical evidence to complete and improve Latin texts that derived from them. The result was an entirely new approach to literary criticism, which was now undertaken for its own sake without reference to the social and political interests of earlier humanists.

It is also largely thanks to Poliziano that the Medici library acquired so many important manuscripts during Lorenzo de' Medici's lifetime – especially scientific, as an exhibition of books in the library on 'The Rebirth of Science' in 1980 demonstrated. It included Euclid's *Elements of Geometry*, acquired by Cosimo from the humanist Filippo Pieruzzi and given to the library at San Marco, with another from the library of the merchant Antonio Corbinelli; Archimedes, copied in Venice at Poliziano's behest for Lorenzo de' Medici; Galen, bought by Poliziano from Paolo Toscanelli's heirs and then translated by him; Pliny's *Natural History*, acquired from Lubeck by Cosimo de' Medici at Niccoli's behest; a tenth-century manuscript of Celsus, *On medicine*, acquired from Milan by Francesco Sassetti, manager of the Medici bank and used by Bartolomeo Fonzio for the *editio princeps*, the very first printed edition, in 1478; Theophrastus, *The History of Plants*, copied by Paolo Toscanelli from an 'ancient exemplar' and emended by Niccoli; Niccoli's copy of Lucretius's *On the nature of things*, which Poggio had discovered in Fulda in 1417; Plato; Aristotle; Ptolemy – one has only to read the catalogue to see how many manuscripts the library contains that are fundamental to the early phases of the scientific revolution [131 *pp. 136–40*].

Poliziano benefited from the 'three momentous changes' – as Anthony Grafton calls them [82 *p. 14*] – that influenced humanists after the middle of the fifteenth century: first, the new libraries in Rome and Florence; second, the invention of printing that 'made possible a new precision in textual scholarship' by enabling humanists throughout Italy to have uniform copies of classical texts to work from; and lastly, confidence gained from assimilating the work of earlier humanists. The importance to him of Niccoli's library is clear from the passage in which he explains his method for establishing correct texts [*Doc. 10*]. Yet although for many historians the study of ancient texts is the most important and long-lasting achievement of the Renaissance, the recovery of the books that encouraged it had other important results.

9   NEW SCHOOLS

Petrarch's passion for books in turn fed other new enthusiasms, the most important of which was new schools with new teaching programmes. Although he wasn't a teacher himself, the subjects he cultivated – history-writing, poetry and literature, letter-writing and internalised debates on personal and ethical subjects – were all humanist, or liberal-arts subjects, as opposed to the more skills- and science-orientated subjects of the medieval teaching curriculum. So too was art, which Petrarch also encouraged, more portraits of him surviving, as we saw, than of any of his contemporaries. By writing in Italian as well as Latin, he helped to feed the new intellectual public that was developing in Italy's cities and courts, enthusing them as well as other scholars with his personal passions. The scholars provided the know-how – it was they who recovered the ancient books that told them about classical schools and teaching programmes and then put them into practice – and this new intellectual public provided the institutional backing and the pupils, without which nothing would have changed.

Two classical books were particularly influential, neither known about in Petrarch's day but rediscovered and translated in the early fifteenth century. One was Quintilian's *On the education of an orator*, preserved in the monastery library of St Gall until Poggio 'liberated' it from imprisonment in this 'gloomy dungeon' in 1417 [*Doc. 9*] and copied it for his friends. The other was Plutarch's *On educating children*, which had been translated into Latin a few years earlier by Guarino Guarini, one of Chrysoloras's pupils (Chrysoloras himself wrote a Greek grammar called *Erotemata* which became an important text in the new liberal-arts curriculum). Together they encouraged the setting-up of new schools and new teachers as well.

The name of the school we know most about speaks for itself about the enthusiasm of its founder: the Casa Gioiosa or Happy School, established at Mantua under the direction of Vittorino da

Feltre (1378–1446). This school has been called by one historian, W. H. Woodward, 'the first great school of the Renaissance' [162 *p. 24*]. It was set up in 1423 by the Gonzaga family in a building surrounded by a large meadow, which had been a gaming house, 'La Giocosa', whose name Vittorino punningly changed to 'La Gioiosa'. Vittorino had been a grammar teacher in Padua and Venice (with Gasparino Barzizza, an early humanist teacher, and Guarino) and was invited to teach the Gonzaga children initially, three boys aged from nine to three years (followed by a girl and another son). But soon he was teaching the sons of leading Mantuan families as well as some poorer children from the city, and also the children of rulers and schólars from elsewhere in Italy (the famous soldier-scholar Federigo of Montefeltro was educated there, as well as the children of the humanists Guarino, Poggio and Francesco Filelfo) – about seventy in all. Pupils were charged according to their means, and the fees and living expenses of the poorer ones were paid by Vittorino himself. Reading and writing were taught to the youngest children by letter games; after a course in grammar, older children learnt to read and declaim passages from Latin and Greek historians and orators, teaching in the two languages proceeding together. Other subjects from the old *quadrivium* like arithmetic, geometry and astronomy were taught in a practical way, arithmetic by games, geometry by drawing and surveying, astronomy by studying the stars. Greek was taught by scholars like Theodore Gaza, whose Greek grammar was later introduced by Erasmus to Cambridge where it helped to popularise this new subject. Although the emphasis was literary, another feature of classical education revived by Vittorino was regular physical exercise. Leaping, running and ball-games were all introduced, to create – as the Latin tag says – 'a healthy mind in a healthy body'. Vittorino himself played an active role in his school, teaching for some seven or eight hours a day and sometimes rousing a pupil from bed early in the morning to give him special tuition.

Thanks to the growing intellectual public for the new ideas, enthusiasm for these new-style schools spread to a milieu very different from the aristocratic court at Mantua, where the sons of *condottieri* like the Gonzaga and the Montefeltro of Urbino were educated. The writer and architect Leon Battista Alberti also recommended the new humanist programme in his dialogue *On the family*, written in Florence in the 1430s. Despite the Florentine origins of his family, Alberti had been educated in Padua by Barzizza and doubtless aimed his book partly at people like the Gonzaga, whom he would prefer to have 'a book' in their hands 'than a sparrowhawk'; but we know it must also have included merchant families like his own from the fact that he also says he has never 'liked the common saying of some people that if you know how to sign your name and can figure out your balance, you have enough education. All our Albertis were educated people' [7 p. 80]. Traditionally, merchant families would destine their children at birth for a business career. After attending a communal or private primary school to learn to read and write, they would spend about two or more years, from the age of ten, at a secondary or 'abacus' school to learn mathematical and commercial skills, before being apprenticed to a merchant firm. Now Alberti suggests that fathers should not decide on their children's careers at birth; instead they should discover their natural talents by watching them at play, and then they should educate them with wide reading – Homer, Virgil, Demosthenes, Cicero, Livy and Xenophon, he suggests – and sports like archery and ball-games. For men are by nature social, created by nature to be active and to live and communicate with others [*Doc. 12*].

The Alberti were one of the richest and most outstanding merchant families in Florence before being exiled in the 1390s. Although Leon Battista had been born in exile and was educated in Gasparino Barzizza's humanist school in Padua (which Vittorino da Feltre also attended), his dialogue represents the ideals of the rich merchant class in Florence. Since the beginning of the fifteenth century men like Niccoli had been spreading enthusiasm for the new humanist programme among members of the merchant class – such as Piero de' Pazzi, whose father was per-suaded by Niccoli to give him a humanist instead of a commercial training, and Matteo Palmieri, an apothecary whose book *On civic life* advocated the same studies. In this climate, Alberti's dialogue fell on fertile soil. Florentine fathers not only copied its advice into their notebooks but they rapidly employed tutors for their children to put it into effect. Lorenzo de' Medici appointed Angelo Poliziano as tutor to his boys and girls. As well as teaching them Greek and Latin, this eminent scholar also found himself playing games with his young charges: 'Our only news', he wrote sadly to their father from the country in 1478, 'is that we are having such continual rain that we cannot leave the house and have exchanged the chase for playing ball, so that the children may not miss their usual exercise' [6 *pp.* 213–14].

What was the appeal of this new education to professional soldiers like the Gonzaga and merchant-bankers like the Alberti and the Medici? On the face of it, Latin, Greek and archery were not the most practical skills for either soldiers or bankers, any more than they were for children elsewhere in Europe where they rapidly became fashionable too – as we can see from Sir Thomas Elyot's *Book Named the Governor* (1531) [*Doc. 13*], and from Roger Ascham's *The Scholemaster*, which warned young nobles that unless they learnt the new 'Italic' handwriting, 'the meaner men's children' would replace them in government [*9 pp. 40–1*]. Historians have assumed that the liberal, republican values professed by humanist education were appealing because they related to the political life of self-governing Italian cities and offered a more secular and 'humane' standard to replace the vocational training of medieval schools. Communications-skills like rhetoric, language and history were obviously useful to self-governing communities where citizens participated actively in politics – as the early appointment of public teachers of grammar and rhetoric in Italian cities suggests. Ancient books on rhetoric and politics had been read since the twelfth century to enable citizens 'to participate in the political life', rhetoric, 'that is, the science of speech', being called 'the science relating to the government of cities' by Brunetto Latini, chancellor of Florence's first popular government. Education and the ability to read silently for oneself is closely linked to political as well as personal independence – 'the condition of autonomy ... the reader's *habeas corpus*', as De Certeau suggestively calls it [in *52 p. 17*]. The same idea was expressed in the fifteenth century by Alberti, who thought education was 'a great help in any activity whatsoever ... There is no need to explain ... how much the knowledge of letters always helps achieve fame and success in whatever one undertakes' [*7 p. 83*]. Nor should poverty be a deterrent: 'Don't for this reason completely give up studying letters', one upwardly-mobile young Florentine wrote to his penniless brother in 1473, 'and don't think that half a ducat more or less in salary per month is what makes you a man.... My advice is that for two or three years, it would be better to you to study, earning money at intervals, than to put up with so much misery.'

But in some ways the new humanist curriculum encouraged less independence than the old scholasticism. By reducing the role of disputation and encouraging the repetitious recital of facts, Anthony Grafton and Lisa Jardine have argued [*85 pp. 23–5*], it was better adapted to creating obedient bureaucrats and courtiers than self-governing citizens. Socially, too, humanism offered a new code of behaviour not only to upwardly-mobile city-dwellers but also to the nobility and their followers as they adapted themselves to post-feudal society. Norbert Elias has defined this change as the transition from an ethos of *courteoisie*, or courtliness, to one of 'civility' or 'civilised' behaviour [68]. Niccolò Niccoli had been one of the first Florentines to establish new standards of 'civilised' behaviour, according to his biographer Vespasiano da Bisticci: 'when he was at table, he ate from the most beautiful antique dishes and the whole table was covered with porcelain and other very elegant dishes. He drank from crystal and other goblets of precious stone. What a noble sight it was to see him at table, as though he were a figure from the ancient world' [28 *p. 402*].

Gradually this new refinement became fashionable in courts and palaces throughout Europe. Whereas previously young men had been told merely 'not to pick your teeth with knives', now humanist instructors like Erasmus told them it was more civilised to 'place your goblet and knife, duly cleansed, on your right, your bread on your left'. In London, the new humanist curriculum was taught at the school founded by John Colet (?1467–1519) after visiting Italy, St Paul's. Although, as Dean of St Paul's, Colet was a clergyman, he did not mind whether the head of the new school he founded in 1509 was a priest or a layman, provided he could teach his pupils 'good clean Latin literature' and Greek if possible. Up to 153 children were to be taught, including poor children who were to pay their way by sweeping the school. Although the curriculum included more religious texts than were taught in humanist schools such as Vittorino da Feltre's in Mantua, Colet's emphasis on classical authors like Virgil, Cicero and Sallust, and his indignant rejection of all 'barbarism' and corrupt Latin marked him as a disciple of the Italian humanist reformers [150 *pp. 83–5*].

So we should not identify Renaissance education too closely with republicanism and individualism – all the less because of its attitude to women. The existence of a few exceptional blue-stockings like Cassandra Fedele in Venice or Alessandra Scala in Florence misled Jacob Burckhardt in the nineteenth century into thinking that Renaissance women 'stood on a footing of perfect equality with men' [44 *p. 240*]. Recent research shows, on the contrary, that they were in some ways worse off than before. Girls as well as boys had been taught to read and write in communal schools in the medieval period, and more women enjoyed scholastic study in convents than in Renaissance courts and universities. Roman law, which was used by most Italian cities, deprived women of independent legal status, and ensured that after marriage women became the possessions of their husbands. So the classical revival in general did nothing to encourage greater equality for women – quite the reverse. The few successful women scholars are famous just because they were exceptions; and successful women politicians, like Eleonora of Aragon and Caterina Sforza, were even rarer. In most cases, Lisa Jardine suggests [92], classical education must have provided women with an extra accomplishment, like music or fine needlepoint, rather than with a necessary skill; and what was true for them might also have been true for men.

Nevertheless, women still had an important role to play as educators, both as teachers (an early children's teacher in Florence was a woman, Clementia) and as mothers. They were largely responsible for the upbringing of their children, and their influence could be crucial in determining the success or failure of the humanist programme. Lorenzo de' Medici's learned mother, Lucrezia Tornabuoni, encouraged it, his aristocratic Neapolitan wife, Clarice Orsini, discouraged it. Clarice was able to get Poliziano dismissed because she disapproved of the new learning and changed the reading of her son Giovanni (the future Pope Leo X) 'to the Psalter, a thing I did not approve of,' – Poliziano wrote to Lorenzo de' Medici – 'while she was absent he had made wonderful progress.' Lucrezia Tornabuoni, on the other hand, was Poliziano's friend and supporter, as well as the confidante of her daughter Nannina, Lorenzo's sister. When Nannina's husband dismissed their children's tutor, Nannina wrote to ask her mother to get Lorenzo to employ the tutor for his young children, doubtless sure of her mother's sympathy when she bewailed the fact that 'it's no use being born a woman if you want to get your own way' [6 *pp. 216, 222–3*]. Aristotle thought women should be educated because they formed half the adult free population 'and from children come those who will become citizens and participate in the political life' (*Politics* I, 1260b). Classical education was most important to the ruling class, and women's special role in the Renaissance, as in Aristotle's day, was to help to rear that class.

10 LOVE OF LIBERTY

'In Florence liberty is no less engraved in men's hearts than it is written on our walls and banners.' The words that Guicciardini puts into the mouth of one of the disputants in his *Dialogue on the Government of Florence* [18 *pp. 16–17*] sums up the love of liberty traditionally associated with self-governing Italian city-states, which did indeed write the word Liberty on their walls and their banners, as Guicciardini says. Traditionally it is another defining characteristic of the Renaissance; for although most of the early communes had succumbed to one-man rule by the fifteenth century, the intense passion for freedom in surviving republics gave Roman republicanism a new lease of life as a burning political issue around 1400 – at least according to the thesis of Hans Baron. However, even in the Renaissance period Florentines like Guicciardini were becoming sceptical about the reality of this liberty, which another speaker in his *Dialogue* describes as 'more a disguise and an excuse' than a natural passion of all men [18 *p. 35*]; and now most historians are equally sceptical, well-aware of the propaganda element in the Florentines' love of liberty and its debt to rhetorical models. Classical republicanism, too, has been redefined and is now recognised as much more elitist and conservative in practice as well as in theory (especially in Plato's and Aristotle's influential writings) than the later progressive and individualistic republicanism of Europe and America [127]. Nevertheless, liberty retained its power to pull the heart strings throughout the period – not only in Italy but also in countries like France and England, where battles for religious and political freedom were encouraging the establishment of republics or 'commonwealths' – and because it was closely associated with the revival of ancient republican ideology, it remains one of the passions that we must investigate and understand.

According to Aristotle, a republican constitution was one in which citizens governed and were governed in turn for the common interest, a system that ensured liberty and equality by frequently changing its office-holders. Italian communes were republican in that government was exercised by a series of very short-term and constantly changing magistracies drawn by lot from those approved as suitable by elected scrutineers – about 10 per cent of the total population. Leonardo Bruni's analysis of the Florentine constitution in his *Laudatio* (*c.* 1402–04) makes this clear. Liberty, he says, was represented by the fact that citizens held government office for only two (or at most four) months at a time, whereas equality was ensured by the fact that all citizens were equally subject to the same laws, and by the imposition of larger fines and penalties on high nobles who broke the laws than on the commoners – in this way compensating the commoners for their otherwise lower status than the nobles [13 *pp. 169–74*]. The extent to which he identified Florence with Greek republics was made even clearer in 1439, when he attempted to explain Florence's constitution to the Greeks attending the Council. It was, he said, 'neither completely an aristocracy nor completely popular but a mixture of both' – in other words, it was like Aristotle's polity, the best practical type of republican government [*Doc. 14*].

Minutes of consultative meetings and books of laws in Florence give a vivid picture of what republican government meant in practice. After informal discussion, when a large number of citizens might be invited to give their views, laws were prepared which were presented first to the popular Council of the People for approval before being ratified by the more aristocratic Council of the Commune. There they were read out, 'clearly and in Italian', and after further discussion, votes would be cast, black beans in the bag for a vote in favour, white beans against. The democracy of this government should not be exaggerated. For although councils normally included a fixed proportion of artisans or minor guildsmen, discussion was nearly always dominated by a few confident and powerful men – as we can see from surviving records, as well as from the fact that in 1475 it was necessary to pass a law ensuring the right of all citizens to speak their minds openly, 'without any suspicion or fear of correction'. Nevertheless, even though many citizens remained silent in meetings, as voters they were all susceptible to the power of rhetoric, on which political success or failure might depend.

The importance of rhetoric, or the art of speaking clearly and persuasively, is evident from the minutes of political meetings in Florence. From the early fifteenth century onwards, we find citizens adopting persuasive techniques learnt from Cicero and Quintilian – using verbs like 'encourage', 'ask', 'persuade', 'criticise' and 'praise' – to get their policies accepted or rejected [43 *p. 10*]. And in 1451 one young

Florentine, the twenty-year-old Donato Acciaiuoli, decided to hold on to his borrowed copy of Cicero's *De oratore* and to give up studying the more advanced subjects of logic and philosophy because he had heard that Carlo Marsuppini was about to give a series of lectures on Greek oratory and poetry. We can only guess why he wanted to change subjects, just as we can only guess why the young Pierfilippo Pandolfini was enthralled by hearing the Greek teacher, Giovanni Argyropoulos, expounding Plato's *Meno*. Both young men were being educated for the political role they would later play in the city, and we can see from the orations that they delivered as members of the government how much they had been influenced by the oratory and philosophy they had imbibed as students in Florence.

Enthusiasm for classical history also had a practical political purpose. Coluccio Salutati's letters often underline a point with a classical reference. The example of Pyrrus, King of Macedonia, was quoted to urge Italian communes to be vigorous in expelling foreign invaders, and that of Scipio Africanus to warn against the danger of engaging in war unnecessarily. By the fifteenth century ordinary citizens were also beginning to appeal to history to bolster their arguments. The massacre at Cannae described by Livy was invoked in one political meeting to argue for a tough and uncompromising attitude towards Ladislas of Naples, then attacking Florence; while Seneca provided an argument for adopting a principled course of action, 'for only that which is honest is good'. Already in 1413 a citizen proposed the axiom that Machiavelli made famous a hundred years later: 'to administer public affairs intelligently, it is essential to look into the past in order to provide for the present and the future.' 'With remarkable suddenness', Gene Brucker comments in his description of these meetings, 'history had become a staple dimension of Florentine political deliberations' [43 *p. 7*].

On this level there was close identification of classical and contemporary values – or so it seemed. For Coluccio Salutati, the contrast was clear between the classical republicanism he identified with a city like Florence and signorial governments elsewhere. In a letter to Bologna on hearing that the papal governor had been evicted, Salutati congratulated the city for establishing a popular government controlled by merchants and artisans. These are the people in every state, he wrote, who love liberty, equality and justice, who do not boast about the nobility of their blood and want to dominate but 'who rule the republic in turn when called to power and when they return to being private citizens obey the government without reservation' [159 *p. 455*]. By the fifteenth century, Florentines began to represent themselves in portrait busts and paintings as ancient toga-clad Roman statesmen on the model of Cicero. Chancellor Carlo Marsuppini [1399–1453] described in a letter how 'the ancients used not only to bestow high honours on those who delivered their fatherland from slavery into liberty but also to adorn them with statues and public monuments.' This was exactly the reward both he and Bruni, his predecessor as chancellor, received when they were given public funerals and buried in classicising tombs at public expense in Santa Croce, as though they had been Roman citizens. And when Cosimo de' Medici died in 1464 he was honoured posthumously with the Roman republican title of Pater Patriae, Father of his Country [37 *pp. 14–15*]. By the end of the fifteenth century even non-Florentines like the noble Roman lawyer, Mario Salamonio, found it natural to compare Florence with Athens as a model of the best, 'true' republic.

The problem is that the political reality was very far from the ideal, as Guicciardini suggested by calling liberty only 'a name', 'an image' or a 'disguise' by the early sixteenth century. Even in the late 1300s, Salutati's republican propaganda had been countered with the jibe that Athens had been controlled by 'thirty tyrants', just like Florence; and although he quickly riposted that Florence was administered by 'thousands of men', its consultative meetings were in fact dominated by a hard core of almost exactly thirty men, 'the dominant elite', 'a restricted circle of notables', as a recent analysis of these meetings has revealed. By the fifteenth century, government in Florence, as in other communes, was becoming restricted to fewer and fewer men. Far from being the leading citizen in a community of equals, as his republican title of Pater Patriae suggests, Cosimo de' Medici was in fact the architect of these changes, more of a party boss or *padrone* than a father figure [113].

What was true of Florence was also true of the two other surviving republics, Siena and Lucca. In Venice and Genoa government was exercised by a closed oligarchy of merchant-nobles which – as Machiavelli commented in his *Discourses* (I, 55) [20 *pp. 247–8*] – differed from aristocracies elsewhere only in that their duke or 'Doge' was not hereditary but a life-office, and their power was based on trade and commerce instead of land. So they all looked increasingly like princely courts by the end of the fifteenth century. In the 1470s one humanist wrote almost identical treatises for Lorenzo de' Medici and Lodovico Gonzaga, Marquis of Mantua, giving one the title *On the best citizen*, the other *On the prince*. And Mario Salamonio did something similar when he wrote his treatise *On princely rule* for the Medici Pope Leo X, not long after praising Florentine republicanism fervently. This is why historians are now sceptical about the liberty and equality of

Italian republics, regarding them as propaganda put forth by the ruling elite to justify or conceal their growing monopoly of power. This was exactly the type of government Plato commended in his *Republic*, in which power was restricted to a small group of specialists, or 'philosopher-rulers', and the vogue for Plato in Florence at this time tells us a lot about the political changes that were taking place [37 *pp. 215–45*].

Instead of dismissing the idea of liberty as entirely rhetorical, however, as some historians have done, we need to understand why it still had a practical role to play in Italian politics. It served not only as a source of opposition ideology but also as a warning of things to come, as we can see from Francesco Guicciardini's revealing thoughts about tyranny [*Doc. 15*]. Moreover, as we saw in chapter 4, republicanism itself had two faces, an imperialist face as well as a freedom-loving one. Bruni had used Florence's Roman origins to justify her claim to 'dominion over the whole world', and so did later Florentines, who argued that 'following the precedent of the Romans, whose language we use', the state should be allowed to override individual interests.

This recognition of the overriding interest of the state – or 'the reason of state' as Francesco Guicciardini was the first to call it in the early sixteenth century [*Doc. 35*] – marked perhaps the most revolutionary change in political thinking at the end of the medieval period, for it implied that politics were no longer subject to Christian morality. As early as 1300, the Dominican teacher Remigio de' Girolami had already accepted the implications of the classical view of the overriding importance of the state. For if men are dead, 'forms of stone' as he called them, when their city is destroyed, they must be prepared to sacrifice even their lives for their country, *pro patria mori*. Patriotism helped to provide a new ideal to replace the chivalric and Christian crusading ideal – which, as Florence discovered to her cost, directly conflicted with her commercial interests by prohibiting trade in the East in the later fifteenth century. 'The greatest good and the most pleasing to God is the good one does for one's country,' Machiavelli reminded the future Pope Clement VII, Giulio de' Medici, in his *Discourse* of 1520 (cf. [*Doc. 34*]); and Guicciardini agreed that one should love one's country more than one's soul, because it is impossible to govern states 'as they are held today' according to Christian precepts [*Doc. 35*]. The classical revival, by popularising republican ideals as widely as it did among the ruling classes of Italian cities, played an important part in this revolution in political thinking.

The structure of northern monarchies was very different from Italian communes, but the growing role of elected assemblies in them may be one reason why Aristotle and the experience of Italian republics became increasingly relevant to them. Another reason was the political and religious crises of the sixteenth and seventeenth centuries which challenged the traditional basis of these monarchies, depending as they did on sacral theories of authority and rule by divine right. The language of classical republicanism provided a valuable alternative to these theories, especially its idea of the state as a public affair, *res publica* or 'commonwealth', whose health or political 'interest' overrode religious and moral considerations. Thanks to the new translations and printed editions of Plato and Aristotle, these authors, as well as Machiavelli and Guicciardini, became increasingly popular. Although Machiavelli was not translated into English until the next century, we know how popular he was from his rating in England: topping his list of favourite Italian authors, he was described by one enthusiastic reader in 1500 as 'Matchiavell a great man' [17; 125]. The same ideas were equally popular in France, as we know from the book written by Jean Bodin (*c.* 1529–96), a member of the new French party of flexible politicians (the *politiques*). Entitled *La République* (1576) and in English – when it was translated thirty years later – *The Six Bookes of a Commonweale*, it rapidly became essential reading for all men of letters [10]. The speed with which the new ideas were spreading can be seen from the fact that even before its English translation, 'you can not steppe into a schollar's studye but (ten to one) you shall likely finde open either Bodin de Republica or Le Royes Exposition upon Aristotles Politiques' [142, II *p. 300*]. So although Renaissance republicanism is a hold-all for a variety of associated ideas, it was clearly not an empty or 'rhetorical' ideal but played an active part in the politics of the day.

11 LOVE OF ART AND ARCHITECTURE

One of the first Renaissance art-lovers was Petrarch as an early collector of the paintings of Giotto and Simone Martini. Niccolò Niccoli was an early lover of architecture, with his passion for probing ancient buildings, as was Alberti, who thought no-one could be so 'jealous' as not to love Filippo Brunelleschi's dome. What was new was their self-conscious cultivation of art and architecture as a mark of a cultivated man, or 'art-connoisseur' – as Petrarch reveals in his comment on Giotto in his will: referring to his own painted Madonna by Giotto, he wrote that its beauty 'the ignorant do not comprehend, while masters of art find it wonderful' [158 p. 223]. Once again, he throws light on another Renaissance achievement, the creation not only of works of art but also art-lovers, men cultured enough to appreciate and patronise them.

From this point of view, the art loved and imitated by the humanists reflected their own highbrow tastes and enthusiasms. This, as Martin Kemp says, has tended to 'skew our attention towards the exceptions rather than the norms' [97 p. 52]. Now our focus is being redirected towards less familiar centres and workshops, which produced works of art and artefacts that are as skilled and beautiful as the better-known canon of Renaissance paintings [157]. But since I am pursuing a different theme in this chapter – that is, art as a constituent element in the Renaissance love of antiquity and its programme for revival – I shall follow the humanists' trail to see where it leads us.

The idea of art connoisseurship took off in the fertile circle of Niccoli, which gives itself away with its language of passion and enthusiasm. Niccoli personally knew Filippo Brunelleschi, the leader of this artistic group as an architect, sculptor and active politician in the city. Gombrich speculates that it may have been Niccoli who fired Brunelleschi with an interest in the antique, as the man parodied in 1413 for trying to expound the laws of architecture, who 'probes ancient buildings, surveys the walls, diligently explains the ruins and half-collapsed vaults of destroyed cities ...' [77 p. 78]. Niccoli also encouraged the sculptors Donatello (1386–1466), Luca della Robbia (1400–82) and Lorenzo Ghiberti (1378–1455), and his circle of friends was responsible for commissioning the most important buildings and works of art in the city around 1400. As guildsmen they were in charge of the upkeep of the cathedral and the baptistery, they contributed to the embellishment of the oratory of Orsanmichele, and they also initiated new projects like the Foundling Hospital of the Innocenti. It was in these buildings that the new Renaissance style emerged from the 1420s onwards, encouraged by the taste and enthusiasm of Niccoli and his friends who commissioned them.

The most striking achievement was the construction of the great dome of the cathedral that still dominates Florence today. It was this that overwhelmed Leon Battista Alberti when he saw his ancestral home for the first time in 1434: 'What man however hard of heart or jealous', he exclaimed in the preface to his treatise *On painting* which he dedicated to Brunelleschi, 'would not praise Pippo the architect, seeing so vast a construction here, raised above the skies, broad enough to cover all the people of Tuscany with its shadow' [8 *p. 33*]. Brunelleschi's achievement had been to vault a wider space than had ever been covered before, thanks both to his own inventiveness and to the influence of a classical model, the circular Pantheon in Rome. From the Pantheon he got the idea of building concentric circles of stone. His own invention was to make the rings a mixture of bricks and stones, the stones resting on an octagonal drum to form eight sturdy ribs of stone; he then created an inner as well as an outer dome to help to support the weight of this vast structure. He also designed the apparatus needed to haul building materials, as well as wine, to his workers: no wonder contemporaries admired his engineering skill. When Brunelleschi died, he was buried in the crypt of the cathedral he had made so famous and was later commemorated with a bust and plaque on the walls of the nave: civic endorsement, if it were needed, of his humanist friends' admiration for his achievement.

During the 1430s and 1440s a galaxy of talent worked in the cathedral: Ghiberti made a bronze shrine and stained-glass windows; Donatello made statues of Old Testament prophets and the lively Cantoria or organ tribunes now in the Opera del Duomo; Luca della Robbia made terracotta reliefs; and Andrea Castagno (1419–57) and Paolo Uccello (1397–1475) painted portraits of Florence's famous *condottieri*. The work of all these artists was commissioned by ordinary citizens acting as *operai*, or members of Boards of Works; and it may have been due to the wide consultative process encouraged by guild patronage, Margaret Haines suggests, that a knowledgeable and enthusiastic public for the new art was created, resulting in commissions like the earliest example of perspective *intarsia* (inlaid woodwork) in the cathedral's sacristy [89]. Another novel guild enterprise was Brunelleschi's hospital for orphans and unwanted babies, the Innocenti, commissioned by the rich Silk Guild of Florence in 1420. Although eminently practical (it provided a stone basin or basket with a bell where new-born babies could be left anonymously at night), the hospital was adorned with a beautiful portico, the first Renaissance arcade in proportion and details that became another trend-setter. Other classical buildings followed: the sacristy of San Lorenzo, a parish church that gradually became dominated by the Medici family, and the chapel commissioned by their rivals, the Pazzi, in the Franciscan church of Santa Croce, one of the most perfect Renaissance buildings in its proportions and classical atrium.

Brunelleschi's most revolutionary achievement, however, had nothing to do with architecture but with painting. After returning from a visit to Rome with the young sculptor Donatello in 1410, he set up an experiment so novel that all his friends talked about it: a painting of the octagonal Baptistery from within the west doorway of the cathedral opposite it, using the doors as frames to enclose his painting. When it was finished, he made a small hole in the back of the painting, placed a mirror opposite it, and got his friends to look through the hole to see his painting reflected in the mirror opposite, in this way forcing them to look at the scene from a single viewpoint. Although Ptolemy's *Geography* had contributed to Brunelleschi's new theory of linear perspective [64 *p. 104*], it was this practical demonstration of perspective that caught the imagination of his circle of friends, who then became its principal practitioners.

One of the first was Donatello, in his bronze relief of Herod's banquet in the baptismal font in Siena (from the mid-1420s) and in the later pulpits of San Lorenzo in Florence, as well as in his marble *Ascension* in the Victoria and Albert Museum in London, whose relief is so shallow that the sense of space and depth he creates is extraordinary. Ghiberti followed him with his second set of gilded bronze doors for the Baptistery cast between 1426 and 1452. The contrast between these doors and his north doors, cast between 1403 and 1424, shows the impact of the discovery of perspective. Although Ghiberti had defeated his rival Brunelleschi in the competition for the north doors in 1402 (and we know from his *Commentaries* how proud he was of his victory [*Doc. 28*]), by 1424, when they were completed, they were beginning to look distinctly old-fashioned. The result of adopting the new perspective in the shallow, chased panels of the east doors impressed not only his contemporaries but sixteenth-century artists and sculptors like Michelangelo Buonarroti (1475–1564) and Bartolomeo Ammannati (1511–92), who admired and copied them themselves.

In the field of painting, it was Donatello's friend Masaccio (1401 – *c.* 1428) who applied the new theory to achieve the same realistic effect. His revolutionary painting of the *Trinity* in the Dominican church of Santa Maria Novella must have amazed the parishioners when it was unveiled in 1427, so realistically did it portray a classicising chapel on the flat wall surface. 'It seemed' – as one art-historian has put it [107 *p. 1*] – 'as if someone had knocked a hole in the wall and built a niche in it.' If we look carefully, we can still see traces of the grid Masaccio used to help him work out the vanishing point (or what Alberti later called 'the centric point'), defined at exactly the height of the average viewer, 1.75 metres from the ground.

A year or two later Masaccio developed these techniques further in the frescos he and his older partner Masolino (*c.* 1383–1447) were commissioned to paint in the Carmelite church in Florence. These too broke new ground in applying rules about the horizon line to give unity to all the figures in the painting. Within this mathematically-constructed framework the figures are able to stand in space, giving them the appearance of independence and the *gravitas* that we associate with Renaissance portraiture and sculpture. But although Masaccio and Masolino worked in collaboration in the 1420s (their frescos being completed in the early 1480s by Filippino Lippi, 1457–1504), recent cleaning reveals how different the two men were, as different as Brunelleschi and Ghiberti. Masaccio's heavily sculptured figures and weighty buildings mark him out as a disciple of Brunelleschi and Donatello, whereas Masolino, like the early Ghiberti, still belonged to the more refined and gracious international Gothic style.

Another Florentine painter influenced by the new theory was Paolo Uccello – 'how sweet a thing perspective is', he is reputed to have said. The frescos of the Flood that he painted around 1445 in the cloister of Santa Maria Novella show how the new perspective could be used to give dramatic effect to narrative scenes – even though his attempts at foreshortening in his portrait of Sir John Hawkwood and his battle of San Romano paintings for the young Lorenzo de' Medici (now divided between the Uffizi, the National Gallery and the Louvre) are less convincing. Another was Piero della Francesca (before 1420–92) from Borgo San Sepulchro, a town in south-eastern Tuscany. Borgo retained a lively cultural life after being acquired by Florence in 1440 and it illustrates the dynamic relationship that could exist between subject towns like Borgo and Arezzo, 'on the periphery' of the state, and their overlords, 'in the centre'. This relationship enabled Piero to enjoy a wide circle of patronage, many of his paintings being commissioned by patrons and confraternities in and around Borgo (including the *Trinity* now in the National Gallery in London), while the *Flagellation of Christ*, which best illustrates his interest in perspective, was commissioned by Federigo of Montefeltro for his palace in Urbino, where it remains today. Piero also wrote a book on perspective, *De prospectiva pingendi*. This in turn stimulated a series of books by Luca Pacioli, also from Borgo, on the relevance of mathematics and proportion to practical subjects like double-entry book-keeping and lettering. Luca's *Summa arithmetica, geometria, proportioni et proportionalita* was printed in 1484, which quickly spread these ideas to a new class of artisans and craftsmen.

With the exception of the last two painters, all the artists described above – 'the sculptor Donatello ... Nencio, Luca and Masaccio' – were singled out for praise by Leon Battista Alberti in the Italian version of his treatise *On painting*, which he dedicated to Brunelleschi in 1436. Despite his family roots in Florence and admiration for the city, however, Alberti was born the illegitimate son of an exile, educated in the humanist school of Gasparino Barzizza in Padua and at the law school in Bologna before becoming a papal secretary, arriving in Florence just in time to celebrate the completion of Brunelleschi's great dome. His only building commissions in Florence (apart from the rotonda in SS Annunziata) were for the Rucellai family, for whom he designed an innovative classicising palace, the chapel of San Pancrazio and the marble upper façade of Santa Maria Novella, still boldly inscribed in Latin with the name of its patron, 'Iohannes Oricellarius'. Otherwise, Alberti worked mostly for princely patrons and for the papal court after its return to Rome in 1443, being closely involved in Nicholas V's programme of restoration and rebuilding.

His princely patrons included Sigismondo Malatesta of Rimini, for whom he audaciously copied the city's Roman triumphal arch in redoing the church of San Francesco as the Tempio Malatestiana [*Doc. 29*]; and the Gonzaga of Mantua, for whom he redesigned the churches of San Sebastian (unfinished) and the magnificent Sant'Andrea, with its lofty round arches and a ceiling *a cassettoni* on the Roman model. It was to Lodovico Gonzaga that he dedicated the first Latin version of his book *On painting*, whose preface leaves out all reference to the achievements of the Florentines included in his preface to Brunelleschi, referring instead to painting as one of the liberal arts and hoping that the marquis, as a man of letters as well as arms, would have time to read it [*8 pp. 32–35*]. *On painting*, like Alberti's later treatise *On architecture* (1452), is important for integrating practical experience with analysis of classical theories of perspective and building [143]. It also set new standards for painters in insisting that they should be trained in the liberal arts in order to paint narrative pictures – its description of how Apelles used a dialogue by Lucian to paint Calumny then serving as a model for Botticelli's painting of this subject [*Doc. 17*]. Interestingly, Alberti also wrote his own Lucianesque dialogues and fables that similarly integrated classical models and personal experience to make an original – if ambivalent – statement about life [110 *p. 5*].

Perhaps Alberti shared the same mixed feelings towards Florence as Petrarch, like him the son of an exile who never returned to live in his ancestral home. The artist who most resembles Alberti as a 'universal man of the Renaissance' is Leonardo da Vinci (1452–1519), also illegitimate by birth, though not an exile. Famous as a painter, he, too, was an engineer and writer on scientific and philosophical subjects; his notebooks, written in a secret mirror-handwriting, conceal a wealth of inventions that are still being worked on. After being apprenticed to Andrea Verrocchio (1435–88), according to the traditional Florentine workshop tradition, he offered his services as an engineer and inventor to the Sforza in Milan on the basis of his own inventiveness. He was also the first painter since antiquity to carry out dissections in order to depict the human body accurately – how muscles worked, how babies lay in the uterus – and to make detailed studies of natural phenomena like storms, the behaviour of animals and people who resembled them. He stayed in Milan for seventeen years, playing many different roles as costume designer, hydraulic engineer and court painter, also producing the famous *Last Supper* which (according to Vasari) occasioned his famous comment on artists as men of genius, who 'sometimes accomplish most when they work the least' [27 *p. 263*]. He lived a very peripatetic life after the French capture of Milan in 1499, with sojourns in Mantua (where he drew the portrait of Isabella d'Este which stimulated her wish for something else 'by your hand' [*Doc. 30*]), Venice, Florence and Rome before working for the French court in Milan and France, where he died near Amboise in 1519.

Alberti and Leonardo da Vinci both help to feed the idea of a Florentine-based Renaissance created by men of genius – Alberti by his preface to Brunelleschi, Leonardo by defining the idea of artistic genius – but they also undermine it by the fact that both men worked outside Florence for most of their lives and achieved fame through projects that lay outside the Florentine tradition. They remind us how much the received version of the Renaissance depended on this literary tradition. For this reason, it is important to look beyond Florence to other cultural centres, where different styles of painting were fashionable – such as the rich International Gothic style, that was more favoured at the beginning of the fifteenth century than the starkly intellectual paintings admired by Florence's avant-garde. Even in Florence this style was popular, as we can see from the *Adoration of the Magi* by Gentile da Fabriano (*c.* 1370–1427), commissioned by Palla Strozzi for his otherwise avant-garde chapel in S.Trinità in 1423; and from the Medici's commission to Benozzo Gozzoli (*c.* 1421–97) to paint their palace chapel around 1459 in the same style.

Outside Florence, the most admired painter and medallist was undoubtedly Antonio Pisanello (*c.* 1395–1455/6), a pupil of Gentile da Fabriano, with whom he worked for the papacy in the Lateran Palace a year before Masaccio and Masolino were also at work in Rome. He was employed by all the leading Italian courts – by the Visconti and the Sforza in Milan, by the Este in Ferrara, by the Malatesta in Rimini and by the Gonzaga in Mantua, for whom he painted a room 'of dazzling inventiveness' with Arturian knights wearing glittering silver-painted armour; and finally by the court of King Alfonso of Aragon. He was summoned by Alfonso to Naples in 1449, after Alfonso had heard of his 'many outstanding and virtually divine attributes ... from the testimonies of many people' [97 *pp. 53–54*], designing not only medals for him but also a grandiose triumphal arch [157 *pp. 228, 241–2*]. Gentile and Pisanello are the only two Italian painters included in Bartolomeo Facio's book *On famous Men* of 1456 (together with Jan van Eyck and Rogier van der Weyden from the Netherlands, and Ghiberti and Donatello as sculptors), Pisanello, 'in the opinion of experts', surpassing all others 'in painting horses and other animals' [5 *pp. 173, 177*].

Another widely admired painter was Andrea Mantegna (1431–1506), who worked in Padua before becoming court painter to the Gonzaga family in Mantua. Both cities were centres of humanist learning, thanks to the schools of Guasparino Barzizza and Vittorino da Feltre, and in them Mantegna was also exposed to the influence of Donatello's bronze equestrian statue of Gattamelata (as well as his high altar in S. Antonio in Padua) and to Pisanello's jousting scenes in Mantua. Soon after arriving in Mantua he went on an antiquarian outing to Lake Garda with the well-known humanist collector of inscriptions, Felice Feliciano (1433–*c.* 1479), whose account of the outing explains the mixture of fun and seriousness with which these friends indulged their love of the antique [*Doc. 16*]. The ancient inscription they uncovered later enabled Mantegna to reproduce authentic Roman lettering on the standards and trophies of the famous *Triumph of Caesar* paintings for the Marquis of Mantua (now in the Orangery at Hampton Court in London): another important step in recovering an accurate knowledge of classical times. For it was only now that classical inscriptions and monuments like the Arch of Constantine in Rome were consulted for the details that make Mantegna's painting the first accurate portrayal of the Roman triumph. The success of painters like Mantegna in reintegrating classical subjects and classical forms, for the first time since antiquity, is what Panofsky thinks is distinctive about 'the Renaissance', and why he distinguishes it from other revivals or 'renascences' of Western art [121].

Mantegna was fortunate in having an understanding patron in the third Marquis of Mantua, Federigo Gonzaga, who said that one should take what one could get from 'recognised masters' like Mantegna, since they had their own ideas and should not be given too many instructions [5 *p. 132*]. Since the *Triumph of Caesar* paintings drew the admiration of all his visitors (see chapter 13), Federigo had good reason to be pleased with his painter, whose powerful evocation of an imperial Triumph clearly added to his own prestige as a recently-ennobled *condottiere*-ruler and a discerning patron.

Mantegna's influence was in turn felt in Venice, in the paintings of his brothers-in-law, Giovanni Bellini (d. 1516) and Gentile Bellini (d. 1507), as we can see if we compare the two paintings by Mantegna and Giovanni Bellini of *The Agony in the Garden* in the National Gallery in London. In other ways, Venetian artists like the Bellini and Giorgione (1476/8–1510) are quite independent of developments elsewhere, achieving their effect through colour and intense light effects. The two traditions of painting *all'antica* and painting for colour and light effect came together in the Venetian painter Titian (1487/90–1576), one of the greatest Renaissance artists who has been called a forerunner of the Impressionists for his use of colour. Titian painted not only powerful and realistic portraits but also extremely imaginative and convincing interpretations of classical mythology – such as his moving *The Flaying of Marsyas* in the State Museum in Kromeriz, and *Danaë with Jupiter transformed into a shower of gold* in the Prado, Madrid.

By the later fifteenth century one of the principal centres of art patronage was Rome. It was there that leading painters from Florence and elsewhere were sent to paint Sixtus IV's chapel in the 1480s – Domenico Ghirlandaio (1449–94), Cosimo Rosselli (1439–1507) and Sandro Botticelli (1445–1510), as well as Luca Signorelli (d. 1523) from Cortona and Piero Perugino (bef. 1450–1523) from Umbria. Of the three painters who were recommended to the Duke of Milan around 1490 as having 'proved themselves in the Sistine Chapel', only Perugino, the non-Florentine, was described as 'outstanding'; the other two were Ghirlandaio and Botticelli, who is now best known for his mythological paintings for the Medici circle in Florence, *Primavera, The Birth of Venus* and *Mars and Venus* [*Doc. 31*]. The fourth painter recommended to the duke, Filippino Lippi, had not worked in the Sistine chapel, but – like the others – he had worked for Lorenzo de' Medici and through his influence was employed to decorate the Carafa chapel in Rome. His sojourn in Rome, from about 1488 to 1493, introduced him to the ancient reliefs and grotesques that subsequently made his paintings distinctive; but it was his wide range of styles and his ability to adapt them to the subject matter that made him one of the most respected and sought-after artists in Italy by the time of his death in 1504 [*117 p. 13*].

Drawn by papal patronage, it was also in Rome that a later generation of artists did their best work. Raphael (1483–1520), a pupil of Perugino, rapidly achieved fame for his Vatican Stanze painted between 1509 and 1514: his three famous paintings known as *The School of Athens, The Disputation* and *Mount Parnassus*, which integrate classical arts and philosophy with Christian theology, and the paintings in the Room of Heliodorus. At the same time Michelangelo was producing his unfinished statues for Julius II's tomb and his overwhelming fresco in the Sistine Chapel, the *Creation*, begun in 1508 and completed in 1512. After working for the Medici in Florence in the 1520s on their Library and the New Sacristy, he returned to a changed Rome, producing for the counter-reformation pope, Paul III, his *The Last Judgement* (1536–41) and the Pauline Chapel frescos (1542–50), and for his own tomb the intense *Pietà* (now in Florence Cathedral). With Michelangelo it is generally agreed that Renaissance art had entered a new phase.

The two interweaving themes of this chapter have been artistic achievement in the Renaissance and the enthusiasms of the men who created the tradition of its revival in Tuscany. It was Alberti before Vasari who encouraged the idea of a Florence-based revival of art, but as we have seen, that is only one side of the story, since there were many other important centres and styles of Renaissance painting. Alberti, as an artist and architect, was as aware as the writer Petrarch of the importance of reconstructing or 'refashioning' the past, as we can see from their autobiographies. The idea of self-construction and the 'mutability' of human nature is in itself a fundamental theme in the Renaissance, the last of its defining passions to be explored.

12 SELF-LOVE AND THE RENAISSANCE IMAGE OF MAN

'What a piece of work is a man! How noble in reason! How infinite in faculty! ... in action how like an angel! in apprehension how like a god!' This image of man in Shakespeare's *Hamlet* [II, ii] encapsulates the idealised image of Renaissance man as a microcosm, or little world, portrayed by Leonardo da Vinci as a perfect circle within the larger circle of the world; or by Michelangelo as the material through which the artist releases the divinity latent within it [*Doc. 20*]; or by Pico della Mirandola, in his famous *Oration* on man at the centre of the universe, free to decide his own destiny, either rising to the level of angels or sinking to the depths of animal bestiality [*Doc. 19*]. Consistent with this image of man's independence and freedom was the idea that in Renaissance Italy man became an individual, 'freed from the count-less bonds which elsewhere in Europe checked progress' [44 *p. 171*].

'Humanism' is the word often used to describe this new Renaissance thinking about man and his importance. But humanism was not a coherent system of belief and it did not even exist as a word in the fifteenth century. The word *humanista* emerged in the late Renaissance as student slang to distinguish a liberal-arts student from a civil lawyer (*legista*) or a canon lawyer (*canonista*), encouraging P. O. Kristeller to describe Renaissance humanism principally as the new liberal-arts teaching programme, described in chapter 8 [103; 116 *pp. 8–51*]. Like the word 'Renaissance', 'humanism' was not invented until the late eighteenth or early nineteenth century, and then it was used to describe the movement as a whole. It nevertheless remains useful to describe the values shared by the writers, artists and politicians we are discussing, as long as we remember it was not a word that existed at the time [102].

The word is useful because it suggests that human values were con-sidered more important to these people than the transcendental values stressed by the Church. Their attitude was summed up by the saying of the Greek philosopher and teacher, Protagoras (fifth century BC), 'man is the measure of all things'. This, together with uncertainty about 'whether the gods exist or not', meant that in the absence of a universal standard of right and wrong, morality should be based on a system of human-based relational ethics. For Protagoras and other Greeks, living a moral life also meant living in a state of balance or harmony with the universe, another relativist idea that contrasted with Christian beliefs about original sin and man's inability to lead a good life without God's grace, When these ideas reached Renaissance Italy, they made their influence felt not only in the fields of art and architecture (where Alberti – like Apelles and Protagoras – proclaimed the importance of man-based ratios and values) but also in the fields of education, music and religion. But can we really say that they amounted to a change of outlook and values, a new relativism that changed the way people perceived human nature and man's image?

Like other characteristics of the traditional Renaissance, the image of man's individualism and central place in the universe has been undermined. We are now told that concepts of individualism, or 'the self', were familiar from the thirteenth century onwards, thanks to the innovation of annual confession that encouraged introspective self-analysis. Moreover, Pico's image of man's central place in the universe – we are also told – was anticipated by St Augustine, according to whom man formed the link between the celestial spheres above him, through his spirit, and the four earthly elements below, through his body. It was because Christians like St Augustine inherited so many late-antique ideas about the universe that their re-assimilation in the Renaissance was possible. For ancient philosophers were thought to share an understanding of the same religious truth, as Frances Yates explains in describing how Cosimo de' Medici wanted a manuscript of the supposed writings of the Egyptian magus, Hermes Trismegistus, translated before he died. 'It is an extraordinary situation. There are the complete works of Plato, waiting, and they must wait whilst Ficino quickly translates Hermes' [163 *p. 13*].

So there was no return to paganism in the Renaissance: Christianity remained fundamental to people's lives, both on a spiritual and emotional level and on a social one, for 'ancient religious tradition was in the blood: bred into the bones of men and women ... from cradle to grave'. This is why we have been told, in a recent volume of essays on *Christianity and the Renaissance*, that the two terms, 'Christianity' and 'the Renaissance', should not be regarded as contradictory but 'equal coefficients' in contributing equally to the Renaissance explosion of talent: 'an equilibrium of stimuli – precarious, but at the same time dynamic in its tension between continuity and change' [153 *pp. 2–4*]. Tension may be a helpful concept for understanding the novelty of the Renaissance image of man, since it explains the dynamism generated by the new ideas without suggesting that they necessarily contradicted established beliefs. Just because it isn't always easy to see where the humanists were breaking new ground, we once more need to follow their trail to understand what their new models of behaviour were and why they were admired.

Two classical heroes are particularly useful as our guides, Hercules and Orpheus. Hercules was the tough and courageous hero of classical myth and legend, who although a human was immortalised by the gods for his Seven Labours in slaying the monsters. Another story about him shows he was also admired in the Renaissance for his ability to make the right independent choices when still a young man. This is the story of 'The Choice of Hercules', or 'Hercules at the Crossroads' as it was called, with journalistic flair. It was initially told by a Greek called Prodicus, a contemporary of Socrates in the fifth century BC, to be revived by Petrarch and constantly repeated in the fifteenth century. The young Hercules – the story goes – suddenly came upon a fork in the road. One path was smooth and grassy, leading downhill towards a beautiful beckoning woman, the other (as you might guess) was rough and stony and climbed steeply uphill to an austere and unwelcoming matron. Off his own bat (as you might also guess, otherwise the story would not have been so popular with teachers), he chose the hard and stony uphill path: *per ardua ad astra* (to the stars through difficulty) as the tag has it, since Hercules did achieve stardom in the skies through taking the tougher decision.

Unlike Pico's *Oration*, the story illustrates an important difference between the classical and the Christian view of human nature, or 'man' (this gender word was used generically by both traditions for the human species, so I shall do so too). Christians thought that man, although created in God's image, was corrupted by Adam's sin in eating the fruit from the forbidden tree of knowledge; henceforth he could be saved only by being born again, with a new nature given through God's grace in baptism. So instead of being capable of making free moral decisions, like Hercules, Christian children – even after baptism – needed all the help they could get to avoid the clutches of the devil, as a fifteenth-century painting of the *Madonna del Soccorso* (the Madonna who brings help, or succour, in S. Spirito in Florence) demonstrates, in showing a child being saved from the devil by the Madonna's enveloping cloak.

Ancient Greeks and Romans, however, did not believe in original sin and thought that children's natures at birth were like wax, capable of being impressed with good or bad experiences until they reached the age of discretion. This was the reason, as Plato explained in *The Republic*, why education was all-important and why children should be subjected to no evil influences until their powers of reason had been developed in adolescence. This view was shared by Renaissance teachers and writers like Vittorino da Feltre and Leon Battista Alberti; hence the relevance to them of Prodicus and Plato, as well as educationists like Plutarch and Quintilian. The popularity of Hercules at this time enables us to understand one change in the Renaissance image of man. It is perhaps surprising to find Hercules portrayed on Florence's first communal seal in place of a saint or ruler, and even more surprising to find him sculpted on Giotto's bell-tower in Florence and on one of its cathedral doors. He was there as a model not of Christian virtue but of ancient civic *virtù* or prowess: fearless, brave and self-determining.

Orpheus was another Ancient Greek hero whose popularity in the Renaissance also points to a changing way of looking at man's nature. The myth of Orpheus, like that of Hercules, can be interpreted in many different ways – as it still is today, in films like Cocteau's *Orphée* and *Black Orpheus*. It tells how Orpheus, despite charming the god of the Underworld by his music to release his wife (killed by a snake-bite), nevertheless caused her second death by breaking the god's strict injunction not to look back at her until they reached the upper world. Christians assimilated the myth with the Bible and interpreted it as an allegory about the dangers of looking back, like Lot and Sodom ('No man, having put his hand to the plough and looking back, is fit for the kingdom of God', Luke, 9.62), and also as an anticipation of Christ's harrowing of Hell. For Renaissance humanists, by contrast, the myth was about love and the power of music. Even though its moral – the impossibility of reaching perfection in love, or in life, before first 'dying' – was perfectly compatible with Christian and platonic doctrine (for as St Paul said, you won't live unless you first die, Corinthians I, 15. 35–6), the context in which it was developed suggests that other, more profane aspects of the myth were important in the Renaissance.

In court and carnival plays like Poliziano's *Orfeo*, for instance, Orpheus is dismembered by wild Maenads (following Ovid, according to whom Orpheus abstained from women for three years after Euridice's death and loved boys instead, hence the Maenads' feminist revenge, *Metamorphoses*, 10:83–5) [49]. But it is in the two earliest examples of an entirely new musical form, the opera, that this Greek myth about the force of love and music is fully brought to life again:

Eurydice by Jacopo Peri, written in Florence in 1600, and *Orfeo* by the Gonzaga's court musician Claudio Monteverdi (1567–1643), written in Mantua in 1607. Like the paintings that revived antiquity by reintegrating classical subjects and classical forms, these operas did so by bringing a classical myth together with music that works through our emotions and psyche, not through moral allegory, to make its effect.

In this context, the myth serves to illustrate the revival in the Renaissance of ancient ideas about the influence on our psyche of cosmic harmonies. As a microcosm, man was thought to be influenced by the same musical harmonies as the cosmos, whose spheres reproduced the sounds of the eight notes of the octave as they circled the earth (the ratios of 1:3:5:8 were harmonious, 1:2:9 dissonant). So he was 'balanced' or healthy when in the same state of harmony or balance as the universe. This harmony could be created by buildings constructed according to these ratios, as well as by music, harmonious ratios creating a balanced character, dissonant ones destabilising it. This was why Leon Battista Alberti thought the most perfect churches were round in shape, because they imitated the most perfect geometrical figure, the circle [160 *pp. 27–9*]. So when Brunelleschi's new dome was completed in 1436, the music composed for its consecration by Guillaume Dufay (*c.* 1400–74) corresponded to the ratio of the building itself to intensify its harmony. And for the same reason, a chancellor of Florence, Carlo Marsuppini, wrote in a letter commending one of the city's musicians in 1446, 'Plato ... laid down strict instructions ... about the type of music that should be played, since he believed that if you change the music, you change the ethos of the city' [*Doc. 18*].

Shakespeare was influenced by exactly the same ideas, as we know from *The Merchant of Venice* (V.1), in which Lorenzo tells Jessica about the power of music, 'Since nought so stockish, hard and full of rage But musick for the time doth change his nature'. Although we cannot hear the music of the spheres ourselves in this life ('There's not the smallest orb, which thou behold'st But in his motion like an angel sings ... Such harmony is in immortal souls; But, whilst this muddy vesture of decay Doth grossly close it in, we cannot hear it'), we can nevertheless be moved by it, just as Orpheus moved trees and stones as well as animals by his song – that is, unless we are unbalanced or dissonant characters who are impervious to the moral harmonies of music, for 'The man that hath no music in himself Nor is not mov'd with concord of sweet sounds, Is fit for treasons, stratagems and spoils; Let no such man be trusted. Mark the music.'

So Orpheus provides another key to understanding this new way of understanding man's nature in the Renaissance. As Shakespeare's reference to him suggests, emotions and man's animal nature were now beginning to be viewed more positively, for if animals can be moved by music, they have the potential to be moral beings. By contrast, St Augustine thought that because man was created in 'the likeness of God', it was dishonourable for him to behave like 'beasts ... that are foolish'; although he might succumb to bestiality, he lost his status as a human in doing so. Classical writers, on the other hand, distinguished much less clearly between men and beasts, as the myths of Chiron the centaur (half-man and half-beast), Apollo and Marsyas, and Pan reveal. Fables and bestiaries about animals had been popular throughout the Middle Ages, as well as in classical times, but in books like Aesop's *Fables*, animals usually represent humans and are used to teach moral lessons about human behaviour. But by the later fifteenth century, fables are increasingly used to point out how superior animals are to humans, as we can see from Bartolomeo Scala's short, scathing fable 'Man' [*Doc. 22*], or from Niccolò Machiavelli's poem *The Golden Ass*, modelled on the *Metamorphoses* of Apuleius (b. AD 123). Machiavelli, like Scala, praised animals' bravery and compassion compared with men's, turning upside down the accepted priorities; for in Apuleius the magician is downgraded by being transformed into an ass, just like Ulysses's companions in Homer's *Odyssey* when Circe turns them into swine, whereas the men transformed by Circe into animals in Machiavelli's poem are braver, more temperate and more attuned to nature than they were as men. Similarly, Machiavelli cited the myth of Chiron the Centaur in his more famous book, *The Prince* (ch.18) [*22 p. 99*], in order to emphasise the value of combining animal traits with human ones – especially the fox's craftiness and the lion's strength. Fear, too, became re-evaluated as an important element in human nature, writers like Machiavelli and Hobbes – before Freud – recognising that it could be used as a form of psychological as well as physical control.

Animal craftiness and strength were also qualities that Hercules possessed, suggesting that they may have contributed to the admiration Renaissance people felt for him. Metamorphosis, or the ability to change into different shapes, is another trait admired in the Renaissance, as we can see from these fables and stories. They are only fables, however, and closely influenced by Greek models. There is one account of change that suggests that metamorphosis and loss of identity may also have reflected the social reality of a city like Florence. The story is an account, probably retold by Brunelleschi's biographer

Antonio Manetti, of a practical joke played by the inventive Brunelleschi on a master-carpenter nicknamed Grasso or 'Fatty', who was a bit simple too [*Doc. 21*]. Grasso was punished for his absence from the Sunday evening's supper party of friends by being persuaded that he had become someone else – a fiction that acquired frightening reality through the collaboration of a series of friends, resulting in Grasso's imprisonment and eventual escape from Florence to Hungary, where he won fame and success as master-engineer to Pippo Spano, the king's *condottiere*. So the story has a happy ending that is not fictional, especially since Brunelleschi many years later employed him, claiming credit for driving Grasso out of Florence to win fame and riches elsewhere.

The story was clearly influenced by the myths we have been discussing, for when Grasso asked a fellow prisoner as a well-read man – he was a judge imprisoned for debt – if he had ever heard of anything like his change of identity, he was told, yes, it was nothing new and some had experienced worse: Apuleius had been turned into an ass, Actaeon into a deer, and the companions of Ulysses into animals. Despite this, the story should not be dismissed as a literary construct, since the loss of identity it describes must have been experienced by many new men in Florence, the social mockery they suffered at the hands of the elite being the reverse and less attractive side of man's protean nature and creativity.

Nevertheless, the revival of Greek myths contributed to a shift of emphasis that in the end did help to transform values. The classical figures of Hercules, Orpheus or Chiron provided images for a new understanding of man's nature, a nature no longer crippled by original sin but a malleable mixture of reason and animal passions. By the sixteenth century, medieval vices like anger, sloth, curiosity, negligence and passion itself had been transformed into attributes of creativity and sophistication, if not genius. More importantly, *virtù* had been emptied of its moral content and transformed into Machiavellian 'prowess', a quality much closer to the Herculean *arete* or 'ability' than to the moral *virtue* required of a Christian hero. And flexibility became the quality required to overcome fortune, which was identified by Machiavelli as a genuine element of hazard and unpredictability in the world, no longer merely an aspect of God's providence that we are unable to see. When Machiavelli admired Chiron and the bold man who can beat fortune 'who is a woman' (*The Prince*, chs 18 and 25) [22 *pp. 99, 133*], preferring the Roman virtues of bravery and magnificence to Christian humility [*Doc. 34*], he was adopting classical values and outlook to criticise those of his own day.

If Machiavelli explains why the amoral qualities of flexibility and animal prowess are to be admired, Shakespeare shows them at work in characters like Iago; at the same time, he lets Hamlet undermine his reflections on man's divinity by the comment, 'And yet man ('this quintessence of dust') delights not me' [II, 2]. So the reverse side of Renaissance self-construction – or self-fashioning, as Stephen Greenblatt calls it – is self-destruction, ambiguity and masking, which appear at this time as other facets of Renaissance flexibility and mutability (as we shall see in chapter 16). Perhaps it is this moral flexibility or freedom to change one's nature, like Proteus, that is the special passion of the Renaissance; for unlike medieval allegories or exemplary lives that represent unchanging moral values, the meaning of Renaissance self-constructed lives constantly changes. The humanists may have seemed copycats in adopting antiquity as their model, but in doing so they created a new language, or 'system of representation', as Chartier calls it, that didn't simply replicate antiquity. This new language spread from its initial urban and courtly environment to ever-widening intellectual circles, until it eventually – thanks to the invention of printing and new Renaissance theatres – reached a much wider populace. How this happened is the subject of Part Four.

PART FOUR: SOCIETY AND THE CIRCULATION OF NEW IDEAS

13 COMMERCE AND THE CLASSICS

How ideas are diffused is not always clear. It used to be thought that they were spread mainly by books, as the means through which their authors' ideas were transmitted to a passive reading public. This is why the recovery of classical texts played such an important role in the traditional account of the Renaissance. Now it is argued that the process is two-way – or better, circular, since by imposing their own interpretation on what they read, readers actively contribute to the making as well as the diffusion of new ideas. This 'reception theory', according to Peter Burke, in his recent account of how Baldassare Castiglione's *Book of the Courtier* was received in Europe, undermines the conventional story of the diffusion of the Renaissance in two ways: it undermines the idea that the Italians actively created Renaissance culture for consumption by other European countries, which, one by one, passively 'succumbed to its spell'; and it undermines the concept of a received 'tradition' which assumes that there is no difference between what is handed down and what is received [46 *pp. 2–5*]. For these reasons, it is argued, 'circulation' may be a better word than 'diffusion' to describe this two-way process, since it suggests a more equal relationship between the producers and consumers of Renaissance culture.

Circulation, like the words 'producers' and 'consumers', also belongs to the world of commerce, which offers another recent approach to re-interpreting the Renaissance. It was adopted by Richard Goldthwaite in 1993 to describe what he called 'the internal dynamic of change' in the consumer habits developed in the Renaissance [76], and three years later by Lisa Jardine, in a book that describes 'goods in profusion' as the necessary precondition of change [93 *ch. 1*]. The following year Anthony Grafton reminded us, in his *Commerce with the Classics*, that commerce also has an intellectual dimension, in meaning communication, or dealings, with someone (as with God), and that it is used by Valla in both senses (as communication and exchange of goods) to describe the activity of translation as a form of commerce in shifting goods from one mind to another [81 *p. 15*]. And at the same time, Dora Thornton also argued, in *The Scholar and his Study*, that it is difficult to distinguish clearly between material and intellectual culture since the study was both a place for business activities and 'a space for reflection and solitude', its bronze inkwells jostling for space with antique bronzes, Chinese celadon and highly-prized maiolica [149 *pp. 12–13*]. And so too did Paula Findlen's account of museums and scientific culture in early modern Italy [69], which – as she and Kenneth Gouwens argue in the 1998 issue of the *American Historical Review* (pp. 51–124) – vindicates the Renaissance as a joint material and intellectual (or 'cognitive') re-living of ancient culture.

The important issue that all these historians address is the relationship between ideas and their material context, which the language of commerce and exchange may describe better than the language of patronage alone, which has the disadvantage (from the currently-fashionable viewpoint) of describing a one-way and downward process of the commissioning of artefacts by patrons rather than an open and circulatory distribution of goods. Or, as it is commonly believed, 'the artist articulates ... the message assigned by the patron' [73 *p. 392*]. These two languages in turn reflect contrasting views of culture, one the 'high culture' of commissioned works of art, which was what used to be meant by Renaissance culture, the other the 'material culture' of the profusion of everyday (but luxurious) goods now thought to typify it.

The links of art and patronage with commerce in banking and trading centres like Florence and Venice are obvious, even if understated until now. Not only did the merchant mentality encourage the acquisitive instinct 'to see and to acquire', as Gregorio Dati put it, 'so that whoever is not a merchant and hasn't investigated the world and ... returned with possessions to his native home is considered nothing' [*Doc. 7*]; it also encouraged the pleasures of spending, as Giovanni Rucellai admitted in saying that 'it is even more pleasurable to spend than to earn' [*Doc. 23*]. More practically, banks provided the funding – as well as a means of transport – for books and art-objects bought overseas and in Italy [*Doc. 32*]. The account books of the Salviati Bank (now in Pisa) are a rich source of evidence for payments to artists and sculptors like Michelangelo and Giambologna (1529–1608), while the Strozzi and Ridolfi banks financed printing enterprises in Venice. Banks also acted as places of safe-deposit for jewels and jewellery entrusted to them as securities for loans – such as the Papal tiara, which was held by the Medici bank on the death of Innocent VIII as security for the huge loan made by the Medici and other bankers to the papacy, or Cardinal Francesco Gonzaga's cameos, retained by the Medici in settlement of their loan to him of 4000 ducats, which Piero de' Medici in turn gave as security to the Chigi bankers in return for a loan to him [93 *p. 422*]. The money gained from these loans was often spent on buildings and art-works – the Chigi bankers spent it on a luxurious villa in Rome, land, jewels and tapestries [74 *pp. 95–6*]. As a result, big cities like Florence, Venice and Rome combined the means and the motive to spend. Lisa Jardine cites the rich commodities to be found in the shops of international merchants like Francesco Datini of Prato or the Venetian Francesco Barbarigo [93 *pp. 103–4*], which in turn encouraged ostentatious spending on culture by wealthy patrons. And Creighton Gilbert documents market sales of paintings in Florence and Venice as early as the late fourteenth and fifteenth centuries [73 *p. 407*].

In fifteenth-century Florence, this wealth triggered a competitive cycle of palace and chapel building, with all the domestic and liturgical apparatus that this involved. It began with the novel classicising chapel and tomb commissioned by Palla Strozzi in S. Trinità after the death of his father in 1418, which in turn provoked Cosimo de' Medici and his brother to imitate him in S. Lorenzo, and it ended in the 1490s with the palace built by the Strozzi at a cost of some 40,000 florins in emulation of the 'marvellous' Medici and Pitti palaces, built during their absence from Florence in exile. The patrons of these buildings were all members of Florence's ruling-elite. They were not all new men or *arrivistes*, as Bill Kent says, since they came from old-established banking and trading families as well as from new families, but they all aspired to a distinctive, and increasingly aristocratic, social and cultural identity and they used the new classical language and style to achieve it [99 *pp. 51–54*].

Venice was the city that most resembled Florence in its commercial wealth, republicanism and size, and its growing empire and prosperity also encouraged a programme of cultural renewal in the fifteenth century. Unlike Florence and most other Italian cities, however, it lacked Roman origins and it was also isolated from other centres of culture – despite Petrarch's visits to the city in the mid-fourteenth century and its close contact with humanist teachers like Gasparino Barzizza in Padua. As Patricia Fortini Brown has demonstrated, Constantinople, not Rome, provided its cultural model and its legitimising trophies [41 *p. 131*]. But although slow to take off, its programme of renewal gradually drew it into the cultural orbit of other Italian cities:

a fresco cycle of the legend of Alexander III in the Doge's Palace by Gentile da Fabriano and Pisanello, a series of triumphal gateways, classicising medals and monumental tombs to memorialise the Doges, combined with official histories and a public library to house the codices of cardinal Bessarion. Bessarion's will shows the influence of Niccolò Niccoli and Pope Nicholas V in wanting a home for his books 'that is both safe and accessible, for the general good of all readers', but he was original in choosing Venice as the most convenient site for Greeks like himself, since of all the nations who 'flock in vast numbers to your city from almost all over the earth, the Greeks are most numerous of all' [42 *pp. 102–115, 145*].

So by the late fifteenth century Venice finally became the new Athens, capital of an intellectual empire that boasted classically-trained scholars and printers like Marcantonio Sabellico (1436–1506) and Aldus Manutius (1450–1515), artists like Jacopo Bellini and his sons (*c*. 1400–70/1), Titian and Tintoretto (1518–94), and architects like Jacopo Sansovino (1486–1570) and Andrea Palladio (1508–80). Patronised by the nobility, they established a new classical model both for public buildings and confraternities (*procuratorie* and *scuole*) and for private palaces and Palladian villas that was later imitated all over Europe and then in America. Machiavelli, as we saw, thought Venice was unusual in restricting power to an aristocracy of some two thousand nobles, headed by an elected Doge, and for being founded on trade, not on land with castles and 'jurisdiction' over men. It was also unusual in the number of its foreign residents – as Bessarion points out – which made it an ideal centre for diffusing the new print culture in which bankers had early on invested. So it provides an excellent illustration of the way commerce contributed to the circulation of the new Renaissance culture – even though – or perhaps because? – Venice had no classical past to revive.

The distinctively urban and professional culture of cities like Venice and Florence remained independent of 'both the political control and culture of courts' until at least the seventeenth century, as Dora Thornton argues in describing the phenomenon of the urban study. Nevertheless, as she recognises, it is impossible in practice to isolate urban intellectual space from that of courtly environments, since the private study of a Florentine banker like Giovanni de' Medici – with its marble inlay and twelve marble heads of the Caesars, encouraging as Amanda Lillie says, his self-image as an Ancient Roman – was not in essence different from Federigo of Urbino's self-idealising study, with its *trompe-l'oeil* intarsia inlays [149 *pp. 8, 51, 120– 1*]. As patrons both were equally rich, since soldiers like Federigo da Montefeltro earned as much as 60,000 ducats a year in peace-time and 80,000 when fighting. Yet despite their wealth and fighting skills, their employers treated them like 'peasants', as Federigo complained to his fellow *condottiere*, Ludovico Gonzaga, in 1461 [56 p. 70]. So they had the motive as well as the money to convert their earnings into cultural assets, such as palaces, libraries and paintings – and even when governments were unable to pay their soldiers, the compensation offered to them could also boost spending on culture, as when Florence repaid its debt to the Gonzaga by allowing them to endow a chapel in SS Annunziata [3 pp. 114–16]. The story of cardinal Francesco Gonzaga's cameos, which were used as security for cash loans and also as collectors' pieces, shows that it is as difficult to separate commerce from culture as it is to separate the patronage of courts from that of city elites.

The patronage of the Gonzaga in Mantua illustrates this very well [56 pp. 143–71]. Mantua was already the home of the first Renaissance school, and in 1441, after the ennoblement of the first marquis in 1433 and Alberti's dedication to him of his treatise *On painting*, Pisanello was invited to paint in the palace his brilliant mural of jousting knights. It seems to have been the ecumenical council held in Mantua in 1459 that triggered a second burst of artistic activity. Perhaps, as Howard Burns says, it was just because Mantua was 'not a state of the first importance' [48 p. 27] that Lodovico, the second marquis (who ruled from 1444 to 1478), invited Alberti to build the magnificent church of S. Andrea, and Mantegna to become his court painter. In the forty or more years Mantegna worked in his court, he produced a series of paintings that put Mantua on the map and also helped to bring fame and prestige to the Gonzaga themselves. His magnificent *Triumph of Caesar* paintings, Lodovico's grandson told the artist, gave the family 'glory in having them in the house' [66 p. 15], while his frescos in the Camera degli Sposi glorified the family by memorialising them for posterity. By including portraits of his overlord, the emperor, and a relative, the king of Denmark, Lodovico also showed his awareness of their importance as publicity – whose effectiveness was evident not only from the Duke of Milan's chagrin at being excluded from 'the most beautiful chamber in the world' that everyone 'here is talking about', but also from Lodovico's unwillingness to remove what had been 'seen by so many people' [5 pp. 130–1].

Other visitors to the palace included ambassadors and lords, whom Lodovico also sought to impress with his culture, as we know from the reason he gave for liking one of Mantegna's architectural drawings: that 'frequently ambassadors and lords come and to honour them one seeks to show them stupendous works, and I will now have this marvellous drawing to show' [48 *p. 27*]. Another visitor was Ercole d'Este, the Duke of Ferrara, who saw the *Triumph of Caesar* paintings at an early stage and 'liked them very much' [66 *p. 22*], while Lorenzo de' Medici especially enjoyed 'certain heads in relief with many other ancient things' [5 *p. 133*]. Since Lorenzo was himself the owner of a fine collection of antique gems and was also a patron (like his grandfather Cosimo) of the new classicising architecture, we can assume that he shared the Gonzaga's motives for wanting to be associated with antiquity. By incising his name on his ancient gems and vases, he also ensured that this association would be long-lasting.

The collecting of antiquities continued in Mantua after the marriage of Ercole d'Este's daughter Isabella to Francesco Gonzaga in 1490. Isabella d'Este (1474–1539) was an exceptional patron of the arts, by her own admission just as *appetitosa* (hungry) for art as any man, especially classical art, for which she confessed she had 'an insatiable desire'. She commissioned paintings for her *Studiolo* from Mantegna, Perugino, Correggio and Titian – failing only with Giovanni Bellini and Leonardo da Vinci (who drew her portrait instead). She also acquired precious objects for her *Grotta*, adding medals, vases, figurines and statues to her collection of cameos, which totalled 1,241 items by the end of her life. For this reason she has been called 'the first Renaissance woman to have been involved seriously in collecting antiquities' [70 *p. 55*].

As Ercole d'Este's daughter, she must have acquired her passion for antiquities from her uncle Leonello, as well as from her mother, Eleonora of Aragon, who had been brought up in the rich court at Naples [56 *pp. 45–66*] – where humanists like Lorenzo Valla and the artist Antonio Pisanello worked – and was a patron of art in her own right. Leonello d'Este (1407–50) had been taught by Guarino Guarini, the humanist friend of Vittorino da Feltre, and his son Battista, thanks to whom he became an enlightened collector of antiquities and patron of art, employing Pisanello and Jacopo Bellini at his court, as well as the humanist Angelo Decembrio. By introducing Alberti to this cultural circle – during Ferrara's brief moment of international fame in 1438, when at least a thousand Westerners and somewhat fewer Greeks descended on the city for the ecumenical Council that later moved to Florence – he helped to encourage Alberti's interest in statuary and architecture, and it was at Leonello's urging that Alberti embarked on his study of Vitruvius and his own famous treatise *On Architecture*. Leonello also patronised northern artists like Roger van der Weyden and northern musicians like Guillaume Dufay (*c.* 1400–74), laying a basis for the flowering of Ferrarese culture under Ercole d'Este (ruled 1471–1505) and his wife Eleonora [*56 pp. 119–142*].

From Ferrara, humanist passions and appetites spread to other Italian courts, not only to Mantua but also to Milan, where Isabella's sister Beatrice presided over the court after her marriage in 1491 to Lodovico il Moro (1451–1508) [*56 pp. 93–118*]. It was doubtless through her that Isabella met Leonardo da Vinci, who worked in Lodovico's brilliant court as his architect, engineer and painter, one of his most admired paintings being of Lodovico's mistress, Cecilia Gallerani, the famous *Lady with the Ermine* which Isabella wanted to see [*5 p. 142*].

At Rimini, another *condottiere*-ruler, Sigismondo Malatesta (1417–68), caught the bug and commissioned a splendid memorial from Leon Battista Alberti. Sigismondo was never ennobled (on the contrary, he was excommunicated and canonised to hell for his military behaviour), but perhaps this made it all the more imperative to immortalise himself and his mistress Isotta in a grandiose reconstruction of the church of S. Francesco [*Doc. 29*]. Incorporating the triumphal arch, Corinthian columns and ornamental disks from the Arch of Augustus in Rimini, Alberti's success in creating a monument to the glory of Sigismondo can be seen in the medal struck of the 'temple' in 1450 by Matteo de' Pasti, who gave it the name by which it is still known, the Tempio Malatestiana.

But of all these *condottieri* courts, the most outstanding was that of Federigo of Montefeltro in Urbino. Educated in the new Gonzaga school at Mantua, Federigo was perhaps the richest and most successful soldier of his day, and yet lacked political legitimacy (he was created duke of Urbino only in 1474). Thanks to his patronage, Urbino was transformed from a small hill-town into a cultural centre of lasting importance, the setting of Castiglione's famous *Book of the Courtier* which evokes the 'enlightened and cultivated atmosphere' of Urbino under Federigo's son Guidubaldo [*56 p. 66–91*]. He used his money to build a beautiful Renaissance palace in Urbino which still survives. The books procured for his distinctive library by Vespasiano da Bisticci now form part of the Vatican Library, but Vespasiano's affectionate biography of his patron [*28 pp. 84–114*], together with Piero della Francesca's portrait of him and his wife Battista (the daughter of another *condottiere*, in the Uffizi Gallery in Florence), serve to keep alive Federigo's memory as a man of culture – as well as arms – in just the way he must have intended.

All these rulers were closely related by marriage as well as by their military profession. So marriage provided another conduit for the spread of the new culture, as did the political and diplomatic links between *condottieri* courts and urban centres. The flow of envoys not only discussed contracts, payments, leagues and peace but also carried reports on the latest artistic achievements and the best artists. News of Alberti's splendid temple for Sigismondo Malatesta in Rimini was carried to Florence by the city's ambassador in Rimini, and in the 1490s it was an agent of the duke of Milan who acted as a talent-spotter for the duke in Florence [*Doc. 31*]. Artists were also used as instruments of cultural diplomacy, as Caroline Elam has described [67]. Filippo Lippi was sent as a diplomatic gift from Giovanni de' Medici to Alfonso of Naples in 1457, in order to bolster Florence's new alliance with Naples, just as three Florentine artists (Ghirlandaio, Rosselli and Botticelli) were sent to decorate the Sistine Chapel in Rome in 1481 to placate the pope and bolster Florence's peace treaty with him after the Pazzi War. When Lorenzo de' Medici recommended Filippino Lippi to cardinal Carafa, his motives were dynastic rather than political, but since his go-between was the Florentine ambassador in Rome, diplomacy provided the conduit through which the new culture travelled.

Neither the court of the Aragonese kings in Naples nor the Papal Court in Rome can be described as new centres of art and patronage. Yet there was a sense in which their rulers shared the same incentive to invest in culture as the *condottieri* rulers, since they too had to re-establish themselves in power in the mid-1440s and so also became actively involved in circulating artists and ideas. Alfonso embarked on his programme of cultural aggrandisement after finally defeating his Angevin rival to the throne in 1442, summoning Pisanello from Mantua to build a triumphal arch and make medals that celebrated him as a divine Augustus, 'Divus Alphonsus'. The Papacy too re-established its authority after its long absence from Rome with a programme of cultural renewal. Nicholas V instituted a library and translations of rediscovered Greek writings for scholars, and he employed Alberti to embellish the city with majestic buildings, counting both among the achievements of his papacy [*Doc. 24*]. Sixtus IV (1471–84) reasserted the doctrine of papal monarchy in the frescos he commissioned for the Sistine Chapel (to be completed by Michelangelo) and he too embellished the city with his bridge and encouraged palace-building with a law enabling clerics to bequeath their possessions to relatives. Alexander VI (1492–1503) and Julius II (1503–13) built and decorated the Vatican Palace and the new St Peter's. Although attacked by reformers like Savonarola [*Doc. 26*] and Luther, the Church evidently contributed as much as the laity to the new consumer culture.

As we have seen, commerce underpinned most of the 'collectibles' discussed in this chapter and it provides a useful (if non-evaluative) way of understanding how Renaissance ideas circulated in Italy, pumped along by the shared desire of its urban elites and new rulers for status and legitimacy, and a shared classical culture. What it does not do is describe the variety of channels through which Renaissance ideas spread, which were political and representational as well as commercial. We shall return to the political function of art and patronage as the exercise of power in chapter 17 – that is, the use of images, such as those of imperial Caesar and Roman senators, to impose authority. But first we must investigate how these ideas circulated outside Italy, to countries that lacked Italy's political structures and classical heritage.

14 EUROPE AND BEYOND

The Renaissance passions generated in Italy were soon infectiously transmitted to the rest of Europe and beyond – just as the Black Death had been – by boats, trade, goods and human contact. But whether the story is told in terms of countries, commodities or carriers, at some point contact with Italy was essential for the bug to be passed on. Bruges provides a good example. There had been Italian banks in Bruges since the end of the thirteenth century and it became an entrepôt for the exchange of luxury goods, rich silks and gold-tooled objects that were imported in exchange for tapestries and paintings – like the 'two painted canvases' sent by the banker Lorenzo Strozzi to his mother from Bruges, which she told him she would sell, 'if I had a chance to sell them at a profit', otherwise she would keep one, as well as 'The Holy Face ... for it is a devout figure and beautiful' [*5 pp. 110, 117–18*] [*Doc. 32*]. The famous Arnolfini painting by Jan van Eyck of the betrothal between two Lucchese families in Bruges (in the National Gallery, London), like the altarpiece commissioned by the Florentine Portinari in Bruges from Hugo van der Goes (in the Uffizi, Florence) are examples of works of art specially commissioned by Italian bankers from leading Burgundian painters. Trading links between Italy and Bruges also encouraged the exchange of books for the same mixed motives of profit (chests of books forming part of the cargo of Italian galleys by the late fifteenth century) and scholarly delight. It was shortly after a Medici agent in Bruges had one of Ficino's writings copied for the papal ambassador that Ficino's works were to be found in the library of a Burgundian scholar in Ghent [139]. So it was Ficino who provided contact with the Renaissance bug, even though it was carried through the arteries of trade.

The same is true of Germany, where wealthy imperial cities like Nuremberg, Augsburg and Strassburg produced an artistic as well as a literary Renaissance in the late fifteenth and early sixteenth centuries. In his study of the work of the limewood carvers of southern Germany,

Michael Baxandall demonstrated how conditions similar to those in Italian cities – wealth, new patrons and more independent working arrangements – produced an artistic movement that was analogous though initially unrelated to Italy's. When Italian influence arrived in Augsburg around 1500 through the merchant-banking Fugger family, who had close trading connections with Italy, 'the city's new men had use for both Italianate ideas and Italianate people of various kinds' – including book-keepers who knew about double-entry accounting, and humanist lawyers who could use Aristotle to justify Augsburg copper monopolists, as well as artists [31 *p. 136*]. Hans Holbein (1497–1541) and Albrecht Dürer (1471–1528) were both artists trained in late-Gothic workshops (in Augsburg and Nuremberg) who felt the need to travel to Italy in the early sixteenth century, creating a new German Renaissance art that resulted from many different influences, wealth, metals and Italian know-how.

Hungary was similarly open to the influence of Italian trade and culture. An Italian trading colony had been established at Buda since the fourteenth century, thanks to the dynastic links between Hungary and Angevin Naples, while a counterflow of Hungarian students studied in Bologna and Padua. By the fifteenth century, Italian humanists and artists like Pier Paolo Vergerio and Masolino worked in Hungary, encouraging an influx of Italian humanists and artists during the reign of Matthias Corvinus (d. 1490), who commissioned from the Florentine bookseller Vespasiano da Bisticci a library to rival those of Cosimo de' Medici, Pope Nicholas V and Federigo Montefeltro of Urbino. Since Matthias's successors were also kings of Bohemia and were closely related to the kings of Poland, 'a cosmopolitan humanist central Europe was beginning to take shape'. Bohemia, of course, had been influenced by Italian culture since the reign of Charles IV (1347–78), who invited Petrarch and Cola di Rienzo to Prague, whereas Poland was a later developer. It was the arrival there of an emigré from the paganising Academy of Pomponio Laeto in Rome, Filippo 'Callimacus' Buonaccorsi, in the reign of Casimir IV (d. 1492) that stimulated cultural as well as diplomatic contact with Italy – making Cracow in the sixteenth century the meeting place of humanists from Italy as well as from Germany, the so-called 'sodalitas Vistulana' [123 *pp. 164–220*].

Constantinople is another city where trade provided the channel for the exchange of Renaissance commodities. Venice and Genoa had enjoyed trading privileges with Constantinople since the Fourth Crusade in 1204, but it was after the city's capture by the Turks in 1453 that the trade in luxury goods really took off. This was again a two-way process, the Sultan exporting rich silks, brocades and ceramics for the Italian market in return for the loan of engineers and artists like Gentile Bellini from the Doge of Venice and Matteo de' Pasti from Sigismondo Malatesta. That such exchanges were 'cultural transactions' was made plain by Sigismondo's letter to the Sultan and his other gifts to him: some maps and a copy of a book *On Military Matters* by another member of his entourage, Robert Valturio. In the preface to this book, Valturio explains that the appeal of Matteo's work in the *Tempio Malatestiana* was to 'learned viewers, who are almost entirely different from the common run of people', while Sigismondo in his letter offered Alexander the Great to the Sultan as a cultural model: for according to Cicero, he wrote, 'Alexander the Great, mindful that for enduring greatness his likeness ought to be preserved for posterity, chose only the greatest painters and sculptors for the task' [93 *pp. 231–9*]. In fact, Matteo de' Pasti never reached the Sultan with these useful messages, since they were confiscated by the Venetians in Crete as militarily sensitive material – reminding us that these gifts had an even more practical function. But the incident usefully illustrates the role of trade (and the diplomacy it involved) in circulating the cultural ideas fashionable among Italian urban and court elites.

Expansion westwards towards the New World and southwards to Africa also took place within a context of cultural and gift exchange, according to Jerry Brotton. Far from representing an intrepid and 'civilising' conquest of new horizons, as Burckhardt famously suggested, European expansion westwards towards America and southwards down the Africa coast was primarily a commercial and mutually beneficial enterprise, not a colonising one, in which maps, globes and navigational know-how formed part of the cultural transaction [35 *pp. 19, 27–8*]. In this instance, contact with Italy was provided by a book, Ptolemy's *Geography*. This book played an important role in the traditional account of the Renaissance as the revival of classical antiquity, and since it was in Florence that it was first copied and translated – arriving at 'a particularly opportune moment', according to Samuel Edgerton, 'when the intellectual climate of the city was ripe to take advantage of it in resourceful ways' [64 *p. 114*] – it also seems to confirm Florence's importance as the centre of new ideas. It interested not only artists like Brunelleschi and the mathematician Paolo Toscanelli, but also the merchants who produced copies of the Latin translation a decade or so after it reached Florence. In 1417 a French cardinal bought a copy of Ptolemy in Florence, and an updated version ten years later, at about the same time that the brother of the Portuguese king, Henry the Navigator, visited the city. Moreover, it was in

Florence that a public disputation on Ptolemy's *Geography* took place, one of the disputants, Francesco Berlinghieri, being the first person to produce a treatise on it in Italian (dedicated to the Sultan Mehmet II); and it was from Florence in 1474 that Paolo Toscanelli wrote the letter acquired by Columbus about the narrow western route to the East. But once the *Geography* had been printed in 1477 (in Bologna, six new editions being printed there and at Rome, Florence and Ulm within ten years), the link with Florence was less important, since the book then became as widely available in Europe as it had long been in the East. Viewed from Brotton's wider perspective, Florence's role in transmitting the text is not undermined but subtly revised by appearing as part of a reciprocal process of cultural exchange [35 *ch. 3*].

Turning back to Europe, we can trace the spread of Renaissance ideas by the same mixture of influences – commercial as well as cultural. In England, too, trade combined with the influence of books and individuals to circulate the new culture. In 1475 the printer Nicolas Jenson was asked to provide copies of Pliny's *Natural History* in Italian, with two histories of Florence in Italian, for some Florentine businessmen and diplomats in England. So the following year he despatched eight Plinys and five copies of each of the histories to be shipped in Venetian galleys to the Strozzi agent in London, two years later adding Plutarch to the shipment. By the 1480s, 'this traffic in books became a flourishing trade', supplying English scholars as well as the Florentines in London, and in turn encouraging English printers to compete in the market [93 *pp. 143–4*]. The fact that these Florentines needed a special delivery of books seems to confirm Poggio Bracciolini's account of his visit to England in 1419–20, which gave him 'no pleasure for a number of reasons' but particularly because it had 'no books'. There were, in fact, many old books as well as enthusiastic book-collectors in England – especially the royal family, King Henry IV and his sons Henry (later King Henry V), Humphrey duke of Gloucester, and John duke of Bedford; John created his own library, and, as Regent of France from 1422 to 1435, acquired 843 books from the magnificent library of Charles V of France in the Louvre [146 *pp. 91–6*]. But Poggio's story supports the traditional version (told by Roberto Weiss) of humanism's arrival in England via Poggio and other members of Florence's avant-garde like Leonardo Bruni. For it was after reading Bruni's translation of Aristotle's *Ethics* that Humphrey duke of Gloucester commissioned him to translate Aristotle's *Politics*, which Bruni dedicated to him in 1437. This in turn encouraged the Italian humanist Pier Candido Decembrio to dedicate his translation of Plato's *Republic* to the duke, who then asked Decembrio for help in building up his classical library. Like Niccolò Niccoli, Humphrey was a patron rather than a scholar, being unable to read the Greek manuscripts he had acquired, but by bequeathing his books to Oxford University he is remembered as the patron of what is still called 'Duke Humphrey's Library' in the University's Bodleian Library [155 *chs III, IV*].

The new enthusiasm for learning Greek in turn drew other English nobles and ecclesiastics to Italy, such as the Earl of Worcester and Robert Flemmyng, Dean of Lincoln, who went to Ferrara to study Greek in the mid-fifteenth century. Two other Englishmen went to Florence to study with Poliziano, William Grocyn (*c.* 1446–1519) and Thomas Linacre (*c.* 1460–1524), who both became serious philologists like their teacher; another, John Colet, the founder of St. Paul's School, studied with Ficino in Florence. Sir Thomas More (1478–1535), Lord Chancellor of England, was another enthusiast for Greek and the new humanism, as a pupil of Grocyn and Linacre and a friend of Colet's. He and Colet in turn became friends of the man who, after Petrarch, is considered the model Renaissance humanist, Erasmus of Rotterdam (*c.* 1477–1536).

According to Lisa Jardine, it is Erasmus who best exemplifies the interactive process by which Renaissance culture circulated. For Erasmus's reputation as 'the quintessential European man of letters' was, she argues, the self-conscious construction of a group of scholars, who used letter-writing, printing and portrait-painting – he was painted by Quentin Metsys, Holbein and Dürer – to create and circulate his scholarly image [91 *p. 147*]. Unlike Petrarch, Erasmus was able to use the new invention of printing to create a public audience, but he followed Petrarch in adopting classical literature, portraiture and the device of letter-writing to create his own self-image. Like Petrarch, he inveighed against barbarism, using satires and philological criticism (as editor of Valla's annotations on the *New Testament* [*Doc. 11*]) to attack the abuses of his day.

Illegitimate by birth, Erasmus was educated at the reforming school of the Brethren of the Common Life at Deventer in the Netherlands and at the University of Paris. His literary circle was formed initially in England, by the close friendships he formed in 1499 with Colet and More. Following his visit to Italy from England, Erasmus dedicated his punning *In Praise of Folly* to his friend More (*Encomium Morae*, 'more' meaning 'folly' in Greek). More in turn wrote an equally satirical attack on contemporary abuses in his *Utopia*, published in 1516 in Louvain through the auspices of Erasmus and his editor Peter Gilles, a character in the dialogue. The following year, Erasmus and Gilles sent More a diptych painted by the local painter Quentin Metsys, which represents the two donors both by their portraits and by their books; while More, by contrast, is represented *in absentia* by the letter being written to him and his *Utopia* proffered in the foreground by Gilles.

Among this circle, it was Rudolph Agricola (1443–85) who provided Erasmus with a legitimating (if somewhat indirect) link with Italy, as a former pupil of Guarino's son in Ferrara and a teacher of one of Erasmus's teachers in Deventer. He in turn may have influenced the Spanish humanist Juan Luis Vives (1492–1540), who was already a friend of Erasmus's when he met More in Bruges in 1515. Other humanists who visited Italy in the fifteenth century were the Frenchmen Jacques Lefèvre d'Etaples (*c.* 1450–1536), who embarked on new editions of Aristotle and the Church Fathers after meeting Pico and Ermolao Barbaro in Italy, and Guillaume Budé (1468–1540), who used Valla and Poliziano for his critical *Annotations* on the Roman law *Pandects* (1508). In Spain, Elio Antonio de Nebrija (1444–1522) contributed to the new Polyglot Bible that revolutionised biblical scholarship, after spending ten years in Italy.

The influence of Italy showed itself more obviously in the new taste for Italian art and architecture and in the court pageantry of Burgundy and Tudor England [147]. The classicising tomb that Henry VIII commissioned for his parents from the Florentine sculptor Pietro Torrigiani (in Westminster Abbey, 1512–18), marked the beginning of the new trend. Soon the influence of Italian art and architecture could be seen in the busts, portraits and miniatures of Torrigiani, Hans Holbein and Nicholas Hilliard and in buildings like Cardinal Wolsey's palace at Hampton Court or the royal palace at Hatfield. By the beginning of the seventeenth century, 'the Italian fashion' of building town houses and living in London instead of in the country had affected the gentry so badly that soon 'England will onely be London and the whole country be left waste'. For this reason James I decreed that 'only Courtiers, Citizens and Lawyers' can stay in London and that the builders of new houses be imprisoned [*Doc. 33*]. It is argued by Susan Foister that it was 'contact with the continent and with France and the Low Countries in particular, rather than with Italy' that encouraged art-collecting in England at this time [71 *p. 23*]. Nevertheless, the 'new tastes and new breed of collector' exemplified by Thomas Cromwell, who owned an Italian Petrarch and Castiglione, show that Italy contributed to the trend towards secular art-collecting by a new elite of courtiers and statesmen.

It was in the sixteenth century that an antiquarian movement developed in England as well as in France, influenced by the new learning spreading from Italy. By attacking the old myths of England's origins in his *History of England* (1534), the Italian historian, Polydore Vergil (*c.* 1470–*c.* 1555) encouraged new critical history-writing which was based on the antiquarian researches of people like John Leland and William Camden (1551–1623) – paralleled in France by Etienne Pasquier's use of philological techniques to study French antiquities, which was why, he wrote, 'I have called my books "the researches"' [*95 p. 271*].

In France, a taste for Italian art and architecture was encouraged by the military invasions of Italy by Charles VIII, Louis XII and Francis I. It was Francis I who persuaded Leonardo da Vinci to come to France after seeing *The Last Supper* in Milan in 1515 – and briefly Andrea del Sarto. When he returned home from imprisonment in 1528, he rebuilt the old castle at Fontainebleau as 'a new Rome', a cultural symbol of the new Renaissance monarchy. There, amidst the classical scenes painted by Rosso Fiorentino from Florence, by Francesco Primaticcio from Bologna, and by Niccolò dell' Abbate, who arrived twenty years later in 1552, pageants and masquerades were performed to verse written by members of the *Pléiade*, a group of classicising poets modelling themselves on the Ancient Alexandrian group of the same name. Using Italian and French diplomats as agents, Francis I also became a collector as well as patron of Italian art, acquiring a Michelangelo, a Bronzino and a Titian, as well as sculptures and plaster casts of antiquities which were transformed into bronzes in the royal foundry. In addition he founded a royal college for the study of classical languages (which he vainly invited Erasmus to take charge of), enriched the royal library, and appointed a royal printer. When the French humanist Francois Rabelais (*c.* 1490–1555) described his ideal educational establishment, the Abbey of Thélème, in 1532, it was 'a hundred times more magnificent than ... Chambord or Chantilly', stocked with libraries of 'Greek, Latin, Hebrew, French, Italian and Spanish books', and attended by 'beautiful, well-built and sweet-natured' men and women who lived according to the motto 'do what you will' [*25 chs 55–8*]. We can detect in Rabelais's satire the growing influence of Renaissance models of mixed-sex, liberal-arts education, as well as the influence of Renaissance architecture.

This was the education given to another important French humanist, Michel de Montaigne (1533–92). Since he was a devout Catholic from the provincial nobility who became councillor to the Parlement of Bordeaux, we might suspect that the evident influence of classical ideas on his writings – his admiration for Socrates as 'a citizen of the world', for example – was purely rhetorical. But it seems that his experience of the barbarity of the civil wars in France, combined with the equally new experience of seeing cannibals from Brazil paraded through the streets of Rouen, made him one of the first spokesmen for religious tolerance. For, he wrote, he did not consider that there was anything barbarous about the cannibals, 'except that we all call barbarous anything that is contrary to our own habits'; it was far more barbarous 'to eat a man alive than to eat him dead' [*Doc. 36*]. He also wrote introspective *Essays*, which were as self-conscious as Petrarch's or Erasmus's portraits of themselves but were novel in showing the author with his warts and all, a new, unclassical way of exhibiting the self.

So, as in Italy, novel thinking emerged from a meeting of new experiences and a reborn – classical – language in which to discuss them. The story of the Renaissance outside Italy shows how many passions were shared with Italy: love of the new learning and new schools, love of Italian art and architecture, and love of self. If these ideas travelled throughout Europe and beyond, it was because they had a market, which in turn created a new 'product' – as Montaigne usefully demonstrates. It is a story in which individuals and ideas still have an important role to play. But by describing their interaction as an open, two-way exchange between equals, this way of talking about the Renaissance avoids the old prioritising of its values as a civilising process. The development that best demonstrates this is printing, which helped to circulate Renaissance ideas and also helped to ensure that another such rebirth was unnecessary.

15 THE INVENTION OF PRINTING

According to Francis Bacon, printing was one of the three inventions that transformed the world – a genuine novelty 'unknown to the ancients' (*Novum organum*) [65 *p. 12*]. Printing did not in itself stimulate new thinking, of course, but by enabling new ideas to circulate more quickly and accurately than before, and among a much wider public, it dramatised their impact. As Martin Davies has written in his translation of Columbus's *Letter on the newly-found islands*, 'Few publicity coups have been so well staged as that which greeted the return of Christopher Columbus from the New World in 1493. With an efficiency and power scarcely conceivable in the purely manuscript age from which Europe had just emerged, news of the discovery spread beyond Spain and reached the great towns of the Continent in the space of a few months' [58 *p. 7*]. Four different printing centres, in Rome, Paris, Antwerp and Basel, all printed their own Latin translation of the letter written originally in Spanish, which was printed and circulated in the Iberian peninsula and in the court of the Spanish pope, Alexander VI. Strassburg had a later German edition, and Florence had a popular Italian edition which was put into verse (for reciting by *cantastorie*, professional story-tellers or buskers) by a priest.

So a new invention celebrated a new discovery, the discovery of the New World, and publicised it throughout Europe in a matter of months: an amazing feat, scarcely equalled even today. No other coups were so dramatic, but books like Berlinghieri's *Geography*, first printed in Bologna in 1477 and reprinted in six new editions at Bologna, Rome, Florence and Ulm within ten years, Luca Pacioli's book on arithmetic and proportion, Nicolas Jenson's edition of Pliny's *Natural History* in Italian despatched to England in 1476, and 1,025 copies of Plato produced by the Ripoli press in Florence, all helped to spread new and newly-discovered ideas during the first decades (the 'cradle' or *incunable* years) of printing. Castiglione's *Courtier* (printed in some 62 Italian editions and in many translations in the 1500s and

1600s) popularised an entirely novel type of courtly behaviour in recommending a 'new word', negligent spontaneity or *sprezzatura*, 'which conceals art and presents what is done and said as if it was done without effort and virtually without thought' [46 *pp. 31, 41, 62*]. Printing also helped to distribute books more widely than before. Initially trade followed the same channels as the manuscript market; but the financial incentive to expand in previously untapped areas, such as along the Rhine, in Switzerland and east Germany, brought books to new places. The fact that every scholar's library possessed its Bodin and Aristotle by the later sixteenth century was due as much to the printing press as to the popularity of the books themselves.

Printing also produced greater accuracy, ensuring 'new precision in textual scholarship', as Anthony Grafton said, in describing printing as one of the 'three momentous changes' affecting humanists in the later fifteenth century. Once printed, texts like Valla's *Emendationes* and his *Annotations for the New Testament* were no longer at risk of being corrupted by scribal copying errors, encouraging the production of better, more correct editions. Other changes introduced with printing, like lists of contents and errata, alphabetical indexes and marginal summaries, made printed books more easily comprehensible to a wider public. By providing maps and detailed tables of numbers and figures that could be compared and brooded on at home, printing was particularly important in the field of science and astronomy. Although Nicolas Copernicus (1473–1543) did not live to see the impact of his famous *De revolutionibus* (of which 400–500 copies were printed in the first 1543 edition and again in the second, in 1566), we know that it was owned by 'the majority of astronomy professors in the sixteenth century' and later by such outstanding astronomers as Galileo Galilei (1565–1642), Tycho Brahe (1546–1601) and Johann Kepler (1571–1630) [62 *pp. 69–71*]. By making another revival unnecessary – since, once printed, the classics were never lost again – Elizabeth Eisenstein argues that it was printing that made the fifteenth-century Renaissance different from earlier and later revivals [65 *ch. 5*].

But does this claim too much for printing? For a long time it was assumed that printing encouraged the classical revival by producing more classical books than other kinds of books, but it might well have been the other way round. Printing may have owed its success to the pre-existing book culture, as Martin Davies puts it, the reason why humanists and literate Italians adapted so readily 'to the innovation from the north' being due to their 'long exposure to an active trade in books' [60 *p. 53*] – and in fact the two Germans who brought printing to

Italy in 1465, Sweynheim and Pannartz, went bankrupt six years later because there was not yet a market for their editions of Latin classics. Printers' lists and library catalogues also show that the market was dominated not by classical texts but by popular and religious books: bibles, confessional manuals, religious tracts, vernacular histories and romances, and the widely-circulated broadsheets of prophecies and monsters studied by Ottavia Niccoli [118]. Nor did printing produce better editions straight away, since old versions of books were often printed before texts were revised – as was the case with Ptolemy's *Almagest*, which was first printed in 1515 in the old medieval Latin version, in 1528 in a new Latin translation and only in 1538 in its original Greek [62 *p*. 6].

A study of printing in Strassburg shows that the proportion of humanist books and the classics respectively fell from 17% and 9% in the period 1480–1520 to 10% and 8% by 1570–99, while in the same periods writings in the vernacular and on science respectively rose from 12% and 11% to 21% and 20% [53 *p*. 298]. No comparable study exists for Italian towns, but in the period 1450–1500 we know that Florence, for instance, produced fewer books of scientific interest than most German towns, about half as many as Ferrara, Rome or Milan, and only a tenth as many as Venice [145 tables on *pp*. 322–50]. Florence's weakness in the field of science – as well as in law and theology (only one Bible was printed in this period) – is perhaps to be expected. But the picture painted by Denis Rhodes's catalogue of all books printed in Florence in this period is much more surprising. Standing fourth in the printing league-table in Italy, with a total of about 775 books printed before 1500 as opposed to Venice's 3,000, Rome's 2,000 and Milan's 1,121, Florence printed no editions of Cicero, Livy, Tacitus or the Plinys before 1500; relatively few Latin poets, Servius's *Commentary on Virgil* being an exception; and only one Aristotle (the *Ethics*). On the other hand the *editio princeps* of Plato was printed there in 1484–85 and Homer in 1488, as well as some other Greek texts, numerous sacred plays, sermons and other vernacular writings, including a magnificent *Commentary* on Dante's *Divine Comedy* in 1481 [130].

But although low in the league-tables, Florence is outstanding for the quality and artistic talent of its books and prints [140 *pp*. 8–10]. The Servius was printed by the goldsmith Bernardo Cennini, who executed some of the reliefs in the reredos of the Baptistery in Florence; and the Dante was illustrated with delicate etchings based on drawings by Botticelli. In fact Botticelli's collaboration with the engraver foundered, perhaps because he was summoned to work in

Rome, but he introduces us to a hitherto neglected 'innovation of great consequence for Renaissance art', the invention of the Renaissance print. As David Landau and Peter Pashall tell us in their important book on this subject, the technical skills needed to make both relief and intaglio prints coincided with the exceptional skills of a number of artists, whose 'talent for draftsmanship came to be the accepted measure of artistic brilliance in European art'. Although it is assumed that woodcuts belonged to the lower end of the market and engravings to the higher end, the distinction between the two was not clear-cut, and by the end of the fifteenth century both types of print – by famous artists in the north and south like Dürer and Mantegna – were being collected by discerning patrons in Europe as well as in the East [104 *pp. 1–6, 91–8*].

Since love of books and love of art are two of the passions that characterise the Renaissance, printing may after all be more integral to the movement than league-tables of editions of books alone might suggest. Dürer was one of the artists patronised by Erasmus, who best exemplified – for Lisa Jardine – the interactive process by which Renaissance culture circulated, by means of letter-writing, portrait-painting and printing. As well as helping to circulate this culture, printing also created new centres that actively produced it. The printing houses of Aldus Manutius in Venice [59; 109], the Amerbachs in Basel or Christopher Plantin in Antwerp created a new polyglot household-cum-workshop that took over the function of earlier courts and cities in clustering talent and diffusing ideas [65 *pp. 99–100*]. Enjoying their own communications network, they created a Republic of Letters that was infinitely expandable, thanks to growing literacy and their ability to harness scholarship to protocapitalist wealth and technology – like the Internet today, whose success as a world-wide web similarly depends on the wealth and technical skills of its producers as well as on the computer literacy of its users. There was another equally interactive network through which Renaissance culture circulated, the theatre. Better than either commerce or printing, the theatre demonstrates how the circulation of Renaissance ideas was – in Stephen Greenblatt's memorable phrases – both a process of self-fashioning and an energising process [87; 88].

16 REPRESENTATION AND THE RENAISSANCE THEATRE

According to Stephen Greenblatt, the Renaissance theatre was the place where the charge of energy created by a work of art was transmitted by the players to the audience and back. In combining the idea of a circuit with the idea of interaction between books, actors and audience, the theatre is, like 'commerce', a channel for spreading Renaissance ideas. It also offers a useful analogy for the Renaissance movement itself, which too was generated by books and discoveries and circulated by alternating current between humanists and their audience. There is another important idea connected with both the theatre and the Renaissance that we need to investigate in this chapter, the idea of 'representation'. In Italian, the word itself means a play or a show in which actors 'represent' or play the role of characters, and it is essential for creating the illusion that the theatre is distanced from the reality outside. But although an illusion, playwrights rely on it to exercise power over their audiences – and so do politicians, as Renaissance writers like Machiavelli realised, when he advised a new prince that political success depends on his ability to manipulate the distinction between appearances and reality, because 'men in general judge more with their eyes than with their hands' and are taken in by appearances (*The Prince, ch. 18*), [22 *p. 101*]. So the theatre, with its role-playing and masking, becomes a metaphor for life itself – thereby providing us with a key to understanding a more complicated world, and a more complicated Renaissance, than a straightforward reading of texts suggests.

There was nothing new about the metaphor of life as a 'theatre of the world', *theatrum mundi*, in which we play an allotted part or role. It derives from both classical and early Christian sources, and after being revived by John of Salisbury in the twelfth century, it was used in sixteenth-century Italy, France and England, where in 1599 it was inscribed on the newly-opened Globe Theatre in London [57 *pp. 138–44*]. What was new in this period is the way it was used, no longer to point out a religious moral (as John of Salisbury had used it) but instead to comment on purely human behaviour and performance. There were no theatres as such in John of Salisbury's day, as there were in classical times, although religious or 'miracle' plays – *sacre rappresentazioni*, as they were called in Italy [153 *pp. 361–412*] – were beginning to be performed in churches and public spaces, with carnivals, jousts and tournaments replacing the open-air circuses and arena events enjoyed by the Greek and Roman populace. Although Alberti described the sight of 'temples, theatres and all the buildings embellished by man' as one of the great pleasures of a cultured man [in 37 *p. 281*], interest in the theatre itself followed the revival of Greek and Latin plays – Plautus's *Menaechmi* was performed in Florence in 1488 and around 1493 Sophocles's *Electra* was performed in Greek in the classical atrium of Bartolomeo Scala's town palace in Florence, his daughter playing the title role [152 *pp. 27–30*]; at the same time Poliziano's *Orfeo* and Greek plays (translated into Latin) were produced for court performances in Mantua and Ferrara. This in turn encouraged the writing of 'erudite' comedies in the sixteenth century by Machiavelli in Florence and Ariosto in Ferrara [126] – and the building of theatres in which to perform them.

It was the sumptuous celebrations in 1589 for the marriage of Christine of Lorraine and the Grand Duke Ferdinand de' Medici that transformed this tradition into opera and the theatre as we know it. Two theatres in Florence were remodelled for performances of three different plays, interspersed with 'intervals' or *intermezzi*, the new hybrid art-form that combined singing and dancing with marvels and unprecedented technical effects of 'unbelievable splendour'. As their effects were later used for the first 'true' opera, Peri and Rinuccini's *La Dafne* in 1598, and again for the marriage of Maria de' Medici to Henry IV of France – the Medici Theatre itself influencing the design of the Farnese theatre in Parma and Inigo Jones's theatre for the Stuart Court in England – we can trace a direct link between this performance and later theatres in France and England [137 *pp. 1–2, 182–5*].

Although these celebrations might seem remote from the popular theatre and from the imagery of the theatre as a microcosm of the world, James Saslow shows how fully the populace was involved both in the preparations and in the festivities themselves. An army of builders and labourers was needed to adapt the three-year-old Medici Theatre and another one nearby, other artisans were needed to make the costumes, and numerous musicians were required, while the festivities themselves included jousts, animal hunts and processions that would have involved 'multiple audiences' throughout the city, accustomed as they were to a long tradition of shows and street entertainments [137 *p. 148*]. The same is true of the audiences and the actors of the Elizabethan theatre, which we are told reflect 'the multiple and shifting class relationships that characterise English Renaissance society, theatre and drama' [135 *p. 31*]. So the idea that 'all the world's a stage', as Shakespeare's Jacques says in *As You Like It* (2:7), is not the religious metaphor it had been for John of Salisbury, but derives from the popularity of the theatre itself in the later sixteenth century – as we can also see from Ortelius's use of the image for his new world atlas, the *Theatrum Orbis Terrarum* of 1570, or from Tommaso Garzoni's 1591 world gazetteer of the professions, *Il Theatro de' vari cervelli mondani* (evidently meaning a show-place, like the 'market-place' of his earlier *La Piazza Universale di tutte le professioni del mondo*, 1587).

To unwrap the full meaning of the metaphor, however, we must return to the popular tradition of carnivals in cities like Florence. When Francesco Vettori used the image in a letter to Machiavelli in 1513, for instance, it was these carnivals he had in mind, not the theatre. In order to describe how the duke of Milan's initial elation at the defeat of its French conquerors was succeeded by the dawning realisation that he was now instead in the hands of the Swiss, Vettori compared him to 'our kings of festivals, who as evening draws on think about having to return to being those men they were before' [21 *p. 284*]. Around the same time, Francesco Guicciardini also used the image of role-playing to describe life 'as a comedy or a tragedy', in which 'we don't rate the person playing the role of the master and the king higher than the person playing the role of the servant: what counts is simply who performs better' (*Maxim* 216) [18 *p. 174*; 19 *p. 97*].

The image of performance and masks thus had political overtones in a city like Florence, where citizens dressed up in the regalia of political office and military service, only to 'drop their masks' when they returned to civilian status two or three months later. From early on, the image of masking also implied duplicity and concealment, for despite the apparent openness of life in the city, ritualised ceremonies were knowingly used to convey duplicitous messages to foreign powers. Sometimes victory celebrations were cancelled and sometimes they were instigated to create a false impression of goodwill, 'like those who masquerade in silk and gold and appear rich and powerful, yet when the mask and the garment come off ... are the same persons they were before' [151 *pp. 285–6*]. The element of deception was also present in the masques and 'disguises' of Renaissance *intermezzi*, and in the cross-dressing and ambiguity of so many of the characters in Shakespeare's plays, who not only change roles and sexes but engage in what Kiernan Ryan calls 'gratuitous flights of verbal fancy and manic-digressive equivocation' [135 *p. 119*]. So if this is theatre of life, what does it tell us about real life in the Renaissance?

One thing it tells us is how important performance and behaviour were in the world in which people were on public display as in a theatre – especially in courts. A Florentine in the papal court described how life in Rome was played out 'before the eyes of this blessed court', and Guicciardini later wrote that 'if you frequent the court of a prince, you must keep yourself constantly in view' (*Maxim* 94), [19 *p. 65*]. This in turn involved duplicity and setting more store by appearance than substance, as Guicciardini admitted, in saying that he regretted not learning as a young man how to 'play, dance and sing and other such frivolities ... that seem more decorative than substantial in man', since they help to promote one's reputation and career (*Maxim* 179) [19 *p. 86*]. Self-awareness and self-construction are themes that run through the Renaissance from Petrarch to Pietro Aretino, who not only successfully promoted himself but also unmasked the vices of others – 'the first public relations man, the first gossip columnist, the first journalist', he has been called, since he wrote whatever would sell in the new world of printing, religious tracts, plays and pornography. He wrote sonnets to illustrate the famous book of Renaissance erotica, Giulio Romano's *Sixteen Positions*, as well as ground-breaking and sexually-explicit *Dialogues*, whose dialogue-form and use of satire still leave critics today uncertain how to interpret them [72 *ch. 2*].

The analogy between the theatre and real life also suggests that the literary technique of deconstruction is more relevant to historians than we might think, since poems and dialogues were used to give vent to other voices excluded from conventional and prescriptive writings – such as those of homosexuals, whose hitherto suppressed but widespread culture is being recovered from carefully de-coded poems as well as from legal documents [75 especially *pp. 84–106;* 132]. The same is true of the equally elusive voice of women, which can also be recovered from literary and legal sources, even if they are not written by women – such as Lorenzo de' Medici's story *Giacoppo* [23 *p. 609*], which reflects on 'the great disadvantage of women and great advantage of men' in marriage, since men can decide to marry someone or not, whereas women 'are always at the discretion of others' – which is not dissimilar from Emilia's 'trenchant and impassioned' speech in Shakespeare's *Othello* on the injustice built into marriage [135 *p. 89–90*]. And whereas the writings of Machiavelli and Aretino were censored by the *Index* of the Council of Trent in 1564, the unsettling banter of Shakespeare's women and fools was much more difficult to suppress. So if 'all the world's a stage' on which masks and confused identities abound, the world they reveal is much richer and more complicated than until recently we have been led to believe.

The analogy of the theatre, with its language of masks and disguise, reminds us that representation also had a political function – especially in a republican city like Florence, where citizens masked and de-masked themselves for public office and where deceptive public ceremonials were integral to the conduct of politics. Their political function was acknowledged by Machiavelli, when he suggested that because men are taken in by appearances, they can be manipulated by rulers – as the people of Cesena were by Cesare Borgia, when he chopped his unpopular captain 'in two pieces' and displayed him 'on the piazza, where he still is, and all the people have been able to see him', the message conveyed by this spectacle or representation being that Borgia 'knows how to make and unmake men at his will' [128 *p. 119*]. Other representations of power – such as the imperial Eagle, the lion of St Mark or Florence's Marzocco – were less brutal but no less effective as signifying overlordship when displayed publicly in subject cities, as were the processions and entries of monarchs into newly-conquered towns.

So the image of the theatre and 'representation' has many different connotations. As a microcosm of the world, it portrays the variety of human types and their capacity to change – confirming the importance of self-construction and display as themes of Renaissance culture. As the place where energy was transferred from writers and players to the audience and back, the theatre, like commerce, also served as the circuit for a two-way interchange between players and audience – or between producers and consumers, in the language of commerce. But its political function, in allowing people's credulousness to be manipulated, reminds us that it is not necessarily a two-way process of exchange. As Roger Chartier says, official or state systems of representation are never politically neutral but serve to exert power in the way that Machiavelli – and later Pascal in seventeenth-century France – describe [51 *pp. 5–9*]. Chapter 13 discussed the merits of describing the two-way circulation of Renaissance culture as 'commerce' rather than 'patronage' – since patronage implies the one-way process, whether we are talking about the clout of a *padrone* or political boss, or the cultural commissioning-power of a Maecenas (Virgil's patron). However, we are now in a better position to see its limitations. For although it is currently fashionable to stress the active role of readers and audiences as equal partners in the new cultural movement, they were also subjected to the cultural propaganda of humanists and politicians. And it remains true that the language and images these men promoted did form 'systems of representation' such as Chartier describes, with their overtones of cultural imperialism. Whether these contrasting 'reconstructive and deconstructive' approaches can be reconciled is the subject of the concluding chapter.

PART FIVE: ASSESSMENT

17 DECIVILISING THE RENAISSANCE

Running through all the previous chapters have been recurring themes or ideas – what I have called Renaissance passions – that seem to acquire coherence by their relevance to the wider social and economic environment in which they developed. Self-construction, literacy and communication skills were valuable assets not only to urban elites and court nobility in the post-plague era but also to up-and-coming 'new men' – 'the meaner men's children', as Roger Ascham called them. It was the response of this very mixed group of people to the new ideas that transformed them into a new culture: a consumer-led boom in material goods and possessions that in turn helped to expand and change the old universe. 'Commerce' seems to provide a convincing metaphor for the production and circulation of Renaissance culture in its widest sense of goods and innovative ideas. Yet is there a danger of confident nineteenth-century belief in progress creeping in through the back door, despite the apparently non-evaluative language of this new metaphor? It is useful to return to the discovery of the New World in 1492 and the revisionary writings its 500th anniversary triggered in 1992, since they provide an evaluative critique of the Renaissance absent from the language of consumerism. They encourage an equally rich, but much less civilised, Renaissance – as I argued, as the basis for what follows, in an earlier reassessment of this other Renaissance [36].

Despite the caution now urged against reading 'possession' and 'conquest' as signs of Western imperialism and hegemony [35 p. 57], it remains true that the popular accounts of the discoveries published in 1493 and later, contribute to a triumphalising view of Renaissance culture. Although the date of 3 August 1492 is famous as the day on which Christopher Columbus set sail for America, it is infamously the day following the expulsion of the Jews from Spain, which forced Columbus to sail not from Cadiz, overcrowded with 'Jew-bearing ships', but from the inferior port of Palos, and with inferior sailors. In the same year the first grammar of Castilian was published, the new 'regularised' language in which Las Casas re-wrote Columbus's own vernacular version of his voyage, thereby distancing us at two removes from the Arabic in which the first conversation between the Old and the New World was originally conducted. The year 1492 therefore marks not only the birth of the 'New World' and modernity but also the end of the rich polyglot culture of medieval Spain and the Old World.

The account of the events of 1492 by Maria Rosa Menocai [112] reminds us of the losses, cruelties and incivilities that accompanied the Civilising Process and the Discovery of the World and of Man. Like Greenblatt, we can point out the inadequacy of Columbus's claim to possession on the grounds that he was 'not contradicted by anyone' after making a proclamation (in Spanish) and unfurling the royal standard [86 *pp. 52–60*]. We can also laugh at the Western prejudice shown by Amerigo Vespucci in criticising the natives of South America for their 'most barbarous customs' and eating habits, not eating at fixed meal-times and reclining on the ground, without using 'tablecloths or napkins' [*Doc. 37*] – unlike that model of Renaissance manners, Niccolò Niccoli, who 'at table ate from the finest of antique dishes ... like a figure from the ancient world'. They make the limitations of Renaissance 'civilisation' all too apparent. The importance of the 'Revival of Antiquity' is also diminished by the experience of scholars like the Jesuit José de Acosta, who was led to *laugh* at Aristotle for being so wrong about the Equator, when he discovered that instead of being scorched by heat there, 'I and my companions were cold' [83 *p. 1*], and like Francesco Guicciardini, for whom the voyages of discovery also demonstrated that 'the ancients were deceived in many things'.

One of the defining characteristics of the Italian Renaissance has always been the period's self-image of itself as a rebirth, but now it is exactly this self-image that is under assault for promoting too favourable and biased a view of itself and projecting on to the barbarian 'other' the aspects that it least liked about itself. A new Renaissance must include the dangerous and difficult texts that were recovered but marginalised for not conforming to the Renaissance's own highbrow view of itself, which can provide a valuable starting-point for defining a less 'civilised' but no less rich and innovative culture. A starting-point is provided by the contrast between Niccoli's 'neatness' and polished table manners, and those of the 'Epicurean' layabouts and cannibals of the New World, whose libidinous activities (Amerigo Vespucci told his patron Lorenzo di Pierfrancesco de' Medici) made eunuchs out of their mates [*Doc. 37*]. Although we may want to dispute Vespucci's accuracy, he points up the limitations of the humanist view of the body, in which only the soul was free, the body itself serving only as 'a kind of cart for moving the spirit about'. As Najemy says [115 *p. 255*], the Renaissance betrayed 'a level of worry' about 'the normal life' of the human body that the discovery of the New World, combined with the discovery of new texts like Lucretius, may have helped to overcome, by giving form to their fears and fantasies.

These discoveries in turn gave rise to what Jonathan Sawday calls a new 'culture of dissection' or 'culture of enquiry' that involved poets and writers, artists and executioners, as well as surgeons operating in Renaissance theatres of display, who together refashioned the world around them: hence its relevance to Renaissance culture in its widest sense [138]. To this new body-language the New World made its own contribution, providing both the Paduan surgeon Mateo Colon and John Donne with the image of their lovers' bodies as 'My America, my new-found-land, My kingdome. Safeliest when with one man man'd'; and Thomas Browne with the image of the body as a cannibal devouring itself, 'since what we hate lies deep within us'. And as we saw, America also encouraged Montaigne's relativist comment that cannibalism for survival was morally better than torturing men and then eating them as in the France of his own day [*Doc. 36*]. So cannibalism may have been one powerful taboo that the New World helped to weaken, in turn eroding the traditional barrier between humans and animals.

Animals, like the body, have always provided metaphors for human behaviour, so it is difficult to distinguish their popularity in allegories like Aesop's fables from a genuinely new attitude to animals in the Renaissance. Nevertheless, Machiavelli's admiration for centaurs as a new male model for princes does suggest that the barriers between men and animals were being broken down. So, too, does Luigi Guicciardini's fable about bees, in which he used the recent experience of Ferdinand of Aragon's captain in Gerba to demonstrate how quickly baboons 'ape' human behaviour; for after passing some baboons on his way to fight the Moriscos, he returned to find there were even more of them, 'all standing upright in formation, with long, thin sticks on their shoulders, evidently imitating the infantry's pike'.

The recovery of ancient texts like Lucretius also contributed to this new, 'decivilised' view of human nature. For in his popular but dangerous poem *On the nature of things* attacking religious superstition, Lucretius not only emphasises the importance of the body, without which the mind or soul cannot survive; more importantly he provides a pre-Darwinian account of man's evolution from animals, which – as Piero di Cosimo's paintings demonstrate – make man much closer to animals than the Christian account of their creation in *Genesis* suggests. For Lucretius, as for his Renaissance admirers like Poggio, Scala and Machiavelli, 'civilisation' was not a Golden Age, and its benefits – like paper and printing – were achieved through man's own hard work and cruelty, in 'slaying everything and devouring whatever inhabits the earth, sky and sea'.

Another text that illustrates this more disillusioned Renaissance is Francesco Vettori's little-known diary of his *German Travels*, which includes the stories, plays and conversations that he heard during his travels – illustrating the multivocity of the Renaissance theatre described in chapter 16, as well as the importance of novel experiences and rediscovered texts in creating a distinctive new outlook. Criticised by his brother for writing about such frivolous things, Vettori responded with the destabilising reflection that all writings were harmful, beginning with the writings of theologians and continuing with those of lawyers, orators and poets, to end with historians – including in his list certain 'ambiguous' writers like the much-admired Pliny, Aulus Gellius, Macrobius and Apuleius, as well as equally admired contemporaries like Poliziano, Pontano and Crinito [29 *pp. 38–42*]. After recounting many interesting encounters, as well as a German play, the diary ends by describing a debate about gambling, with the relativist conclusion that all pleasures are the cause of good as well as evil [*Doc. 38*].

The ingredients of Vettori's sceptical and relativist account of the world, like those of the 'decivilised' Renaissance described in New World texts and rediscovered ancient texts, are the same as those that formed the traditional Renaissance: new texts, new discoveries, and new men who provide the impetus for reconstructing themselves and the world they lived in through new images and in a new language. The recent insights discussed in these chapters together provide a more critical – but no less positive – way of interpreting the distinctive culture, if not the civilisation, of the Renaissance period.

PART SIX: DOCUMENTS

Unless otherwise stated, the translations are my own. I give references to other, full versions of the document when these are available.

THE LANGUAGE OF REVIVAL

DOCUMENT 1   THE RETURN OF THE GOLDEN AGE

Our Plato in *The Republic* transferred the four ages of lead, iron, silver and gold described by poets long ago to types of men, according to their intelligence ... So if we are to call any age golden, it must certainly be our age which has produced such a wealth of golden intellects. Evidence of this is provided by the inventions of this age. For this century, like a golden age, has restored to light the liberal arts that were almost extinct: grammar, poetry, oratory, painting, sculpture, architecture, music, the ancient singing of songs to the Orphic lyre, and all this in Florence. The two gifts venerated by the ancients but almost totally forgotten since have been reunited in our age: wisdom with eloquence and prudence with the military art. The most striking example of this is Federigo, Duke of Urbino ... and you too, my dear Paul, who seem to have perfected astronomy – and Florence, where the Platonic teaching has been recalled from darkness into light. In Germany in our times have been invented the instruments for printing books; and, not to mention the Florentine machine which shows the daily motions of the heavens, tables have been invented which, so to speak, reveal the entire face of the sky for a whole century in one hour.

Marsilio Ficino to Paul of Middelburg, 1492, *Opera omnia*, Basel, 1576, reprinted Turin, 1962, p. 944 (974 in revised edition); cf [1], pp. 79–80.

DOCUMENT 2   THE REVIVAL OF THE ARTS

For some centuries now the noble arts, which were well understood and practised by our ancient forebears, have been so deficient that it is shameful how little they have produced and with what little honour ... Before Giotto, painting was dead and figure-painting laughable. Having been restored by him, sustained by his disciples and passed on to others, painting has now become a most worthy art practised by many. Sculpture and architecture, which for a long time had been producing stupid monstrosities, have in our time revived and returned to the light, purified and perfected by many masters. As for literature and liberal studies, it is better to say nothing at all about them than too little. For more than a hundred years those who should have been the leaders and true masters of all the arts have been neglected and no-one has been found to exist who has true knowledge of literature or who can write with the minimum accomplishment, so that everything in Latin written on paper or carved on marble is a rough caricature of what it should be. But today we see our Leonardo [Bruni] of Arezzo sent into the world as the father and ornament of letters, the resplendent light of Latin elegance, to restore the sweetness of the Latin language to mankind. For this reason anyone of intelligence should thank God for being born in these times, in which we enjoy a more splendid flowering of the arts than at any other time in the last thousand years.

Matteo Palmieri, *Vita civile*, ed. G. Belloni, Florence, 1982, pp. 43–4.

DOCUMENT 3   THE REVIVAL OF POLITICS AND LITERATURE

The Latin language was most flourishing and reached its greatest perfection at the time of Cicero. Previously it was unpolished, imprecise and unrefined, but rising step by step it reached its highest pinnacle at the time of Cicero. After the age of Cicero it began to decline and fall as until then it had risen and it was not long before it sank to its lowest point of decline. One can say that letters and the study of the Latin language went hand in hand with the state of the Roman republic. For up to the time of Cicero they increased, and then, after the Roman people lost their liberty under the rule of the emperors (who did not even stop at killing and destroying men of distinction), the good state of studies and letters perished together with the good state of the city of Rome ... Why do I say all this? Only to show that learning and Latin letters suffered similar ruin and decline as the city of Rome when it was annihilated by perverse and tyrannical emperors, so that in the end scarcely anyone with ability could be found who knew Latin. Then the Goths and the Lombards crossed into Italy, barbarous and foreign nations who to all intents and purposes extinguished the understanding of letters, as can be seen from the documents drawn up and copied in those times, which are unimaginably crude and gross. After the Italian people recovered their liberty following the expulsion of the Lombards, who had occupied Italy for 240 years, cities in Tuscany and elsewhere began to revive. Men started studying again and began to refine their coarse style ... Francesco Petrarch was the first person with enough talent to recognise and recall to light the ancient elegance of the style that had been lost and extinguished.

Leonardo Bruni, *Le Vite di Dante e di Petrarca*, 1436, ed. H. Baron, *Humanistisch-philosophische Schriften*, Berlin, 1928, p. 66; trans. in [12], pp.75–7.

DOCUMENT 4   THE REVIVAL OF PAINTING AND SCULPTURE

Although the arts of sculpture and painting continued to be practised until the death of the last of the twelve Caesars, they failed to maintain their previous excellence. We can see from the buildings they constructed that, as emperor succeeded emperor, the arts declined day by day until they gradually lost all perfection of design ... But because fortune, in jest or in penance, usually returns those she has raised to the top of her wheel to the bottom, it happened after the events I have described that nearly all the barbarian nations rose up against the Romans in various parts of the world. Not only did they bring down the vast Roman empire in a short time, but with it Rome itself and with Rome, all its gifted craftsmen, sculptors, painters and architects, leaving the arts – and themselves – buried, submerged among the miserable ruins of that most famous city ... Then in 1013 the reconstruction of the beautiful church of San Miniato sul Monte showed that architecture had regained some of its earlier vigour ... From these beginnings art and design began slowly to revive and flourish in Tuscany ...

I have perhaps discussed the origin of sculpture and painting more extensively than was necessary in this context. I did so, however, not so much because I was carried away by my love for the arts, but because I wanted to say something to benefit and help our artists. Having seen how the arts developed from small beginnings to reach the heights and then from such a noble position crashed to their ruin, like other arts resembling human bodies in that they are born, grow, become old and die, the process by which their rebirth came about can more easily be understood.

Giorgio Vasari, *Le vite*, preface, cf. [27], pp. 32–47.

PETRARCH, WRITER AND POET

DOCUMENT 5   CHANGING ATTITUDES TO CICERO

Francesco to his Cicero, greetings. Having found your letters where I least expected to, after searching long and hard, I read them avidly. I heard you discussing many things, bewailing many things, changing your mind about many things, Marcus Tullius, and you whom I had before known as a teacher of others I now at last have come to know yourself ... O, restless and ever-anxious man, or rather, to use your own words, 'O, impulsive and unhappy old man' [*Ep. ad Octav.*, 6], what did you hope to achieve by so many disputes and useless enmities? Why did you relinquish that leisure so fitting to your age, profession and circumstances? What false splendour of glory involved you as an old man in adolescent fights and after having made you the sport of fortune led you to a death unfitting to a philosopher? ... I mourn your fate, my friend, and feel shame and pity for your mistakes, and together with Brutus, 'I count as worthless those arts in which I know you were so skilled' [Cicero, *Ad Br.* 1, 17, 5]. Indeed, what use is it to teach others, what use is it to orate about virtue if you fail to listen to yourself? Ah, how much better it would have been, especially for a philosopher, to grow old peacefully in the country, 'meditating', as you yourself say somewhere [Cicero, *Ad Att.* x, 8, 8] 'on eternal life, not on this so transitory life', never to have held public office, never to have aspired for triumphs, never to have been inflated about any Catilines! But now all this is in vain. Farewell, for ever, my Cicero. From the world of the living, on the right bank of the Adige, in the city of Verona in trans-Paduan Italy, the 16th of June in the 1345th year from the birth of that God whom you did not know.

Francesco Petrarch, *Familiarium Rerum Libri*, xxiv, 3, *Prose*, ed. G. Martellotti, Milan and Naples, 1955, pp. 1022–4; trans. M. Bishop, *Letters from Petrarch*, Bloomington and London, 1966, pp. 206–7.

DOCUMENT 6   LOVE AND POETRY

Not like a suddenly extinguished light
her spirit left its earthly tenement.
She dwindled like a flamelet, pure and bright,
    that lessens in a gradual descent,
keeping its character while waning low, spending itself until its source is spent.
    Not livid-pale, but whiter than the snow
the hills in windless weather occupying,
only a mortal languor did she show.
    She closed her eyes; and in sweet slumber lying, her spirit tiptoed from its
        lodging place.
It's folly to shrink in fear, if this is dying;
    for death looked lovely in her lovely face.

Francesco Petrarca, *Canzoniere*, trans. M. Bishop in *Renaissance Profiles*, ed. J. H. Plumb, New York, 1961, pp. 11–12.

FLORENCE AND THE RENAISSANCE

DOCUMENT 7   **FLORENTINE PROSPERITY**

One reason [why Florence is more prosperous than her neighbours] is this. Because the city of Florence is situated in a naturally wild and sterile place, no matter how hard it is worked it cannot provide enough for her inhabitants to live off; and because the population has greatly increased, due to the temperate and generative climate of the place, it has for some time been necessary for Florentines to provide for this enlarged population by hard work. So, for some time now they have gone abroad to make their fortune before returning to Florence ... and travelling through all the kingdoms of the world, both Christian and infidel, they have in this way seen the customs of the other nations in the world and have adopted what they favoured, choosing the flower from every part; and in order to be able to follow these customs, they have been filled with an even greater desire to see and to acquire; and the one has increased the desire for the other, so that whoever is not a merchant and hasn't investigated the world and seen foreign people and returned with possessions to his native home is considered nothing. And this love has so inflamed their minds that, for some time, it has seemed that this is what they are naturally born for. So great is the number of talented and rich men that they are unequalled in the world, and behaving as they do, they are capable of increasing their riches indefinitely and achieving status. So it is that their neighbours, although considerably richer and better off in natural terrain, have been content with what sufficed them, without wanting the bother of acquiring more.

Gregorio Dati, *Istoria di Firenze*, Norcia, 1904, pp. 59–60.

DOCUMENT 8   **THE PROGRAMME OF THE AVANT-GARDE**

To impress the crowd with their great learning, they shout out in the square how many diphthongs the ancients had and why only two are known today ... As for *rhetoric*, they love working out how many good orators there were and argue that rhetoric in itself is nothing and is natural to men ... *Arithmetic* they say is the science of misers to enable them to amass riches to enter in their business accounts ... They scoff at *geometry* ... They say *music* is the science of buffoons to please with flattery ... *Astrology* is the science of lying, deceiving fortune-tellers ... *History* for them is a matter of discussing anxiously whether there were histories before the time of Ninus and how many books Titus Livy composed and why they are not all to be found and what mistakes historians made – Valerius Maximus too short, Livy broken up and chronicles too prolix ... According to them, *poets* write fables and corrupt young people with their inventions and fantasies ... They say Plato is a greater philosopher than Aristotle, quoting St Augustine who called Aristotle the prince of philosophers excluding Plato ... *Moral philosophy* evokes the response: Oh, isn't Tully Cicero's account in the *De Officiis* splendid! ... They know nothing about *household economics* but, despising holy matrimony, they live like madmen without any order ... Concerning *politics*, they have no idea which government is better, that of one, the few, the many or an elected elite ... And as for *divine philosophy*, they greatly admire Varro's numerous, well-written books about the religious beliefs of the Gentiles, which they secretly prefer to the doctors of our Catholic faith; and, forgetting the miracles of our saints, they dare to say those ideas were truer than this faith.

Cino Rinuccini, *Invective*, edited in Italian by A. Wesselofsky, *Il Paradiso degli Alberti*, Bologna, 1867, i, ii, no. 17, pp. 303–16 [all the italics are my own].

ASPECTS OF THE MOVEMENT

DOCUMENT 9   QUINTILIAN RESCUED FROM PRISON

You know that while there were many writers in the Latin tongue who were renowned for elaborating and forming the language, there was one outstanding and extraordinary man, M. Fabius Quintilian, who so cleverly, thoroughly and attentively worked out everything which had to do with training even the very best orator that he seems in my judgment to be perfect in both the highest theory and the most distinguished practice of oratory. From this man alone we could learn the perfect method of public speaking, even if we did not have Cicero, the father of Roman oratory. But among us Italians he so far has been so fragmentary, so cut down by the action of time, I think, that the shape and style of the man had become unrecognizable ... By Heaven, if we had not brought help, he would surely have perished the very next day. There is no question that this glorious man, so elegant, so pure, so full of morals and of wit, could not much longer have endured the filth of that prison, the squalor of the place, and the savage cruelty of his keepers.

By good luck – as much ours as his – while we were doing nothing in Constance, an urge came upon us to see the place where [M. Fabius Quintilianus] was being kept prisoner. This is the monastery of St Gall, about twenty miles from Constance. And so several of us went there, to amuse ourselves and also to collect books of which we heard that they had a great many. There amid a tremendous quantity of books which it would take too long to describe, we found Quintilian still safe and sound, though filthy with mould and dust. For these books were not in the library, as befitted their worth, but in a sort of foul and gloomy dungeon at the bottom of one of the towers, where not even men convicted of a capital offence would have been stuck away.

Poggio Bracciolini to Guarino Guarini, trans. P. W. G. Gordan, [11], pp. 193–5.

DOCUMENT 10   THE NEW PHILOLOGY

I have obtained a very old volume of Cicero's *Epistolae Familiares* ... and another one copied from it, as some think, by the hand of Francesco Petrarca. There is much evidence, which I shall now omit, that the one is copied from the other. But the latter manuscript ... was bound in such a way by a careless bookbinder that we can see from the numbers [of the gatherings] that one gathering has clearly been transposed. Now the book is in the public library of the Medici family. From this one, then, so far as I can tell, are derived all the extant manuscripts of these letters, as if from a spring and fountainhead. And all of them have the text in that ridiculous and confused order which I must now put into proper form and, as it were, restore.

Angelo Poliziano, *Miscellaneorum Centuriae primae* (chapter 25), trans. A. Grafton, [82], p. 29.

DOCUMENT 11   BIBLICAL CRITICISM

As I was hunting last summer in an ancient library – for those coverts offer by far the most enjoyable sport – luck brought into my toils a prey of no ordinary importance: Lorenzo Valla's notes on the New Testament. At once I was eager to share it with the world of scholarship, for it seemed to me ungenerous to devour the prize of my chase in solitude and silence. But I was a little put off; not only by the entrenched unpopularity of Valla's name, but by his subject as well, a subject which on the face of it is singularly apt to generate antagonism. You, however, not only lent your weighty support to my decision the moment you had read the book but also began to urge me ... not to cheat the author of the credit he deserved or deprive countless students of such an enormous advantage just because of the angry snarls of a few critics; for you said you had no doubt that the work was destined to be extremely useful ... You also offered your services as patron and defender; let it only be published even though you alone underwrote the risk ...

Tell me what is so shocking about Valla's action in making a few annotations on the New Testament after comparing several old and good Greek manuscripts. After all it is from Greek sources that our text undoubtedly comes; and Valla's notes had to do with internal disagreements, or a nodding translator's plainly inadequate renderings of the meaning, or things that are more intelligible expressed in Greek, or, finally, anything that is clearly corrupt in our texts. Will they maintain that Valla, the grammarian, has not the same privileges as Nicholas [of Lyra (*c.* 1270–1340), a Franciscan teacher at the University of Paris and best-known biblical commentator in the later Middle Ages] the theologian? Not to mention further that Valla is, in fact, included among the philosophers and theologians by many leading authorities; and conversely when Lyra discusses the meaning of a word he is surely acting as a grammarian rather than a theologian. Indeed this whole business of translating the Holy Scriptures is manifestly a grammarian's function ...

Erasmus to Christopher Fisher, 1505, trans. R. A. B. Mynors and D. F. S. Thomson, *Collected Works of Erasmus*, Toronto and Buffalo, 1975, ii, pp. 89–90, 93–4.

DOCUMENT 12   A NEW ATTITUDE TO CHILDREN

Fathers should behave towards their children in the same way [as metallurgists and architects, who investigate the nature of the subsoil before they start work on it]. Every day they should look very carefully at their children's behaviour to see what their most persistent and recurrent traits are, what they like doing most and what they least like doing. This will provide ample evidence of what they are really like. There are no better clues anywhere to such hidden secrets than in men's behaviour and physiognomy, for men are by nature sociable. They are keen and eager to associate with each other and live happily together, regarding solitude as something miserable and to be avoided ... Nature, the best of builders, not only wanted men to live exposed in the midst of other men but she also seems to have imposed on them the need to communicate and share with others – by speech or other means – all their passions and their emotions. Rarely does she allow any of their thoughts or deeds to remain hidden without someone somehow knowing about them... And so by watching his children day by day the diligent father will learn to interpret their every little word and gesture.

Leon Battista Alberti, *Della famiglia*, ed. C. Grayson, Bari, 1960; trans. Watkins, [7], pp. 45–6.

DOCUMENT 13   EDUCATION FOR NOBLES

And it shall be no reproach to a nobleman to instruct his own children, or at the leastways to examine them, by the way of dalliance or solace, considering that the Emperor Octavius Augustus disdained not to read the works of Cicero and Virgil to his children and nephews. And why should not noblemen rather so do than teach their children how at dice and cards they may cunningly lose and consume their own treasure and substance? Moreover, teaching representeth the authority of a prince; wherefore Dionysius, king of Sicily, when he was for tyranny expelled by his people, he came into Italy and there in a common school taught grammar, wherewith when he was of his enemies embraided and called a schoolmaster, he answered them that ... in despite of them all he reigned, noting thereby the authority that he had over his scholars.

Yet notwithstanding, he shall commend the perfect understanding of music, declaring how necessary it is for the better attaining the knowledge of a public weal; which, as I before have said, is made of an order of estates and degrees, and by reason thereof containeth in it a perfect harmony; which he shall afterward more perfectly understand, when he shall happen to read the books of Plato and Aristotle of public weals, wherein be written divers examples of music and geometry.

Sir Thomas Elyot, *The Book Named the Governor* [14], bk I, chs 5 and 7, pp. 18, 22–3.

DOCUMENT 14   FLORENCE'S CONSTITUTION ANALYSED

Since you want to know about the form of our constitution and how it came to be founded, I shall try to describe it to you as clearly as I can. The Florentine republic is neither completely aristocratic nor completely popular but is a mixture of both forms. This can be seen clearly from the fact that the nobility, who are prominent for their numbers and their power, are not permitted to hold office in this city, and this is contrary to aristocratic government. On the other hand those who practise menial trades and members of the lowest proletariat are not admitted to the administration of the republic, and this seems contrary to democracy. Thus, rejecting the extremes, this city accepts men of the middling kind – or rather, it inclines to the well-born and the richer kind of men provided they are not excessively powerful ...

Since the republic is mixed, we can identify some features as popular, some inclining more towards the power of a few. The popular features are the brief duration of the offices, especially that of the Nine [i.e. the Signoria], which does not last for more than two months, and the Colleges [i.e. the twelve Good Men and the sixteen Standard-bearers], which last for three and four months; short-term offices tend towards equality and are popular, as is our veneration and respect – in word and deed – for liberty, which provides the purpose and object of the whole regime. Also the election of the government by lot and not by vote is a popular feature. On the other hand, many features tend towards aristocracy. It seems to me, for instance, it is aristocratic that everything has to be discussed and approved before being taken before the people; also the fact that the Council of the People can change nothing but must simply approve or reject seems to contribute greatly to the power of the aristocrats.

... In the olden days, the people used to take up arms in time of war and fight the city's battles ... then the power of the city rested with the populace and the people were supreme, even to the extent of excluding the nobles from government. Later wars began to be fought by mercenary soldiers. Then the power of the city was seen to depend not on the people but on the aristocracy and with the rich, who provided the republic with money and served it with counsel rather than arms. Thus the power of the people gradually waned and the republic obtained its present form.

Leonardo Bruni, *De Florentinomm Republica,* Latin translation in T. Klette, *Beitrage zur Geschichte und Literatur der italienischen Gelehrtenrenaissance,* ii, Greifswald, 1889, p. 94; cf. [4], pp. 140–4, for a full translation.

DOCUMENT 15   TACITUS AND TYRANNY

If you want to know what the thoughts of tyrants are, read Cornelius Tacitus' account of the last conversations of the dying Augustus with Tiberius. Cornelius Tacitus is very good at teaching the subjects of tyrants how to live and survive under tyranny, and at teaching tyrants how to set it up.

Francesco Guicciardini, *Ricordi* (ser. C, nos. 13, 18), trans. Brown [18], p. 169.

DOCUMENT 16   AN ANTIQUARIAN OUTING

On the VIII day before the first of October [1464], under the rule of the merry man Samuel de Tradate, the consuls being the distinguished Andrea Mantegna of Padua and John the Antenorean [Paduan], with myself in charge and the bright troop following, through dark laurels taking our ease. Having crowned Samuel with myrtle, periwinkle, ivy and a variety of leaves, with his own participation, and entering the ancient precincts of St Dominic, we found a most worthy memorial of Antoninus Pius Germanicus surnamed Sarmaticus. Steering then towards the house of the holy protomartyr [St Stephen, the first Christian martyr], not far from the said precincts we found in the portico an excellent memorial of Antoninus Pius the God, nephew of Hadrian the God, resident of that region [the two inscriptions of Antoninus are of different dates, before and after he had been formally declared a god]. Going on then to the house of the first pontiff nearby, we found a huge memorial of Marcus Aurelius the Emperor; all of these are recorded in the present notebooks ... Having seen all these things, we circled Lake Garda, the field of Neptune, in a skiff properly packed with carpets and all kinds of comforts, which we strewed with laurels and other noble leaves, while our ruler Samuel played the zither, and celebrated all the while.

Felice Feliciano, memoirs to Samuel da Tradate with his biography of the antiquarian Ciriaco of Ancona, trans. C. E. Gilbert, [5], p. 180.

DOCUMENT 17   EDUCATION FOR ARTISTS

I would like the painter to be as well-versed as possible in all the liberal arts, but first I want him to know geometry ... Next, [the painter] should learn to enjoy poets and orators, for they have many adornments in common with the painter. Literary men are full of information about many subjects and will be a great help in preparing the composition of the narrative, whose great virtue consists primarily in its invention – to such an extent that invention alone can give great pleasure without being painted. The description that Lucian gives of Calumny painted by Apelles excites us when we read it. It is not irrelevant to tell it here to advise painters what care they must take in creating inventions of this kind. This painting was of a man with enormous ears, attended by two women, Ignorance and Suspicion. Approaching from the other side was Calumny herself, a woman attractive in appearance but with too scheming a face, holding in her right hand a lighted torch and with the other dragging by the hair a youth whose hands were raised to heaven. Leading her was a pallid and ugly man, with a grim countenance, like someone exhausted by years of service in the field. This was evidently Envy. Two other women were in attendance on Calumny, busy arranging their mistress's attire, Treachery and Fraud. Behind them came Penitence, dressed in mourning and tearing at herself, then chaste and modest Truth. If this story grips you, imagine how much pleasure and delight Apelles' painting must have given! [The Calumny of Apelles was in fact later painted by Botticelli according to Alberti's description, and is now in the Uffizi Gallery in Florence.]

Leon Battista Alberti, *On painting*, III, 53, the Latin text (with a translation) is in [8], pp. 94–6; cf. [5], pp. 70–1.

DOCUMENT 18   THE ANCIENT ART OF MUSIC

There can be no doubt, I think, about how highly the art of music was esteemed by the ancients, who far excel all others in wisdom. To begin with the philosophers, we find that Pythagoras and those who listened to him thought the study of music so important that they attributed separate sirens to every sphere; nor can we doubt that the heavens and all the elements relate to each other according to a certain numerical harmony. How well-suited it is to human talents we can see from the example of children, who from their infancy quite naturally love lullabies and the sound of bells. Influenced by this, some people have believed that human souls form a harmony. Thus Plato, that most wise and almost divine man, not unreasonably laid down strict instructions in his *Laws* about the type of music that should be played, since he believed that if you change the music, you change the ethos of the city. Take Aristotle, who thought the art of music was necessary for the good life. Or take the fact that no Greek was considered sufficiently cultured if he neglected the art of music. Thus Epaminondas and many other civic and military leaders are said to have been adept at playing the Greek lyre. Composers of sacred songs, hymns and divine lauds were also not esteemed unless they could play the lute and lyre. Our sacred ceremonies, too, are accompanied by the organ and other musical instruments.

Carlo Marsuppini, Chancellor of Florence, letter-patent for a German musician, formerly a pipe-player for the city, 1446, Florence, Archivio di Stato, *Missive* 36, fols. 165v–166r.

DOCUMENT 19   MAN AT THE CENTRE OF THE UNIVERSE

God the Father, the supreme Architect ... therefore took man as a creature of indeterminate nature and, assigning him a place in the middle of the world, addressed him thus: 'Neither a fixed abode nor a form that is yours alone nor any function peculiar to yourself have I given you, Adam, to the end that according to your desire and judgment you may have and possess whatever abode, form and functions you yourself shall desire. The nature of all other beings is limited and constrained within the bounds of laws prescribed by me. You, constrained by no limits, in accordance with your own free will, in whose hand I have placed you, shall ordain for yourself the limits of your nature. I have set you at the world's centre so you may more easily observe the world from there. I have made you neither of heaven nor of earth, neither mortal nor immortal, so that with freedom of choice and with honour, as though the maker and moulder of yourself, you may fashion yourself in whatever shape you prefer. You shall have the power to degenerate into the lower forms of life, which are brutish. You shall have the power, out of your soul's judgment, to be reborn into the higher forms, which are divine.'

Giovanni Pico della Mirandola, *On the dignity of man*, trans. E. L. Forbes, [2], pp. 224–5 (with modernised 'thee' and 'thou' forms).

DOCUMENT 20   THE DIVINE ARTIST

The best of artists has no idea that is not contained within a piece of marble itself with its superfluous shell, and this the hand discovers only by obeying the intellect.

Michelangelo, *Rime*, ed. E. N. Girardi, Bari, 1960, no. 151, p. 82.

DOCUMENT 21   DEPERSONALISATION IN FLORENCE

The city of Florence has in the past had many amusing and agreeable men, and especially recently. One Sunday evening in 1409, a group of friends – consisting mostly of men of standing belonging either to government circles or talented masters from various guilds, such as painters, goldsmiths, sculptors, carpenters and the like – found themselves having supper together, as was their wont. They were in the house of Tommaso Pecori, a fine, upstanding citizen, very amusing and clever, who invited them because he enjoyed their company so much. Having had a light supper, they were sitting around the fire (since it was winter time), either in groups or all together, gossiping about various agreeable topics mainly to do with their professions and work. While they were chatting, one of them said, 'What do you make of the fact that Manetto, the carpenter, isn't here?' (this was the person nicknamed Fatty). It emerged that someone had asked him and he had been unable to come, and that was why he wasn't there. This carpenter worked in a shop on the piazza of San Giovanni and he was at that time one of the skilled masters in his trade; among other things, he was renowned for his skill in crowning picture frames and doing the frames for altar paintings, which not every carpenter was then able to do; and he was an extremely entertaining person, like most fat men; he was a bit on the simple side – about twenty-eight years old, large and sturdily built, hence the reason for everyone at large calling him Fatty. But he wasn't so simple that any but the clever could have guessed, since he was not completely stupid. And because he was normally part of this group, his absence that evening gave them material for fantasising about the reason for his absence.

La novella del Grasso legnaiuolo, ed. C. Varese (Novellieri del Quattrocento), Turin, 1977, p. 49.

DOCUMENT 22   MEN AND ANIMALS

When a cunning fox and the generous lion met in the wood by chance, the fox asked the lion, 'Why are you, O Lion, so nervous?' 'Because of man', the lion replied. Then the fox said, 'Are even you, our king, afraid of spectres? I want you to know the ways of man. If you flee, he is bold; if you are bold, he flees. Nor is man a man. He only seems a man.'

Bartolomeo Scala, apologue 'Man', *Apologorum Liber Secundus* in his *Humanistic and Political Writings*, ed. A. Brown, Tempe, Az., 1997, p. 372.

REASONS FOR PATRONAGE

DOCUMENT 23   THE MERCHANT EXPLAINS

I have also spent a great deal of money on my house and on the facade of the church of Santa Maria Novella and on the chapel with the tomb I had made in the church of San Pancrazio, and also on the gold brocade vestments for the said church, which cost me more than a thousand ducats, and on the loggia opposite my house and on the house and garden of my place at Quaracchi and at Poggio a Caiano. All the above-mentioned things have given and give me the greatest satisfaction and pleasure, because in part they serve the honour of God as well as the honour of the city and the commemoration of myself.

It's generally said, and I agree with it, that earning and spending are among the greatest pleasures that men enjoy in this life and it's difficult to say which gives greater pleasure. I myself, who have done nothing for the last fifty years but earn and spend, as I describe above, have had the greatest pleasure and satisfaction from both, and I really think that it is even more pleasurable to spend than to earn ...

I have also derived and derive the greatest satisfaction from a legacy I have made to the Guild of Bankers for an offertory to be made by the said Guild every year with the corporate membership of the Guild in the church of San Pancrazio, with a certain amount of cakes and Trebbiano wine; also for the marriage each year of four girls born and brought up in the parish of San Piero at Quaracchi; and for two lamps to burn day and night in the sepulchre of the said church. These things give me considerable pleasure and satisfaction because they serve the honour of God and the commemoration of myself.

Giovanni Rucellai, memoir dated 1473, *Zibaldone*, [26], I, pp. 121–2.

DOCUMENT 24   THE CHURCH EXPLAINS

Only the learned who have studied the origin and development of the authority of the Roman Church can really understand its greatness. Thus, to create solid and stable convictions in the minds of the uncultured masses, there must be something which appeals to the eye; a popular faith sustained only on doctrines will never be anything but feeble and vacillating. But if the authority of the Holy See were visibly displayed in majestic buildings, imperishable memorials and witnesses seemingly planted by the hand of God himself, belief would grow and strengthen from one generation to another, and all the world would accept and revere it. Noble edifices combining taste and beauty with imposing proportions would immensely conduce to the exaltation of the chair of St Peter.

Death-bed speech attributed to Pope Nicholas V, trans. in P. Partner, *Renaissance Rome, 1500–1559*, Berkeley, Ca., 1976, p. 16.

DOCUMENT 25   PATRONAGE AS EXPIATION

Having attended to the temporal affairs of the city – which inevitably bur-
dened his conscience, as they are bound to burden all those who govern states
and want to play the leading role – Cosimo became increasingly aware of the
fact that if he wanted God to have mercy on him and conserve him in the possession of his temporal goods, he had to turn to pious ways, otherwise he
knew he would lose them. For this reason, it seemed to him – though where it
came from I don't quite know – that some of his money had been acquired
not quite cleanly. Wanting to lift this weight from his shoulders, he went to
talk to Pope Eugenius who was then in Florence. Pope Eugenius had installed
the Observantist Movement in San Marco, and since it wasn't very well
adapted for them, he told Cosimo what he was thinking of, that Cosimo
should spend ten thousand florins on building works to satisfy himself and
unburden his conscience. Having spent ten thousand florins without complet-
ing what was necessary for the monastery, Cosimo finished the job by spending in all more than forty thousand florins – not only on the building but on
the provision of everything necessary to live there.

Vespasiano da Bisticci, from the life of Cosimo de' Medici, *Le Vite*, ed. A.
Greco, ii, pp. 177–8; cf. [32], pp. 218–19.

DOCUMENT 26   PUBLICITY IN CHAPELS

Look at the habits of Florence, how the women of Florence have married off
their daughters. They put them on show and doll them up so they look like
nymphs, and first thing they take them to the Cathedral. These are your idols,
whom you have put in my temple. The images of your Gods are the images
and likenesses of the figures you have painted in churches, and then the young
men go around saying ... 'that girl is the Magdalene, that other girl is Saint
John', because you have the figures in churches painted in the likeness of this
woman or that other one, which is ill done and in great dishonour of what is
God's. You painters do an ill thing; if you knew what I know and the scandal
it produces you would not paint them ... Do you believe the Virgin Mary
went dressed this way, as you paint her? I tell you she went dressed as a poor
woman, simply, and so covered that her face could hardly be seen, and likewise Saint Elizabeth went dressed simply. You would do well to obliterate
these figures that are painted so unchastely. You make the Virgin Mary seem
dressed like a whore ...

Look at all the convents. You will find them all filled with the coats of
arms of those who have built them. I lift my head to look above that door. I
think there is a crucifix, but there is a coat of arms. Further on, lift your head,
another coat of arms. I put on a vestment. I think there is a painted crucifix
on it. It is a coat of arms, and you know [why] they have put coats of arms on

the back of vestments, [it is] so that when the priest stands at the altar, the arms can be seen well by all the people.

Girolamo Savonarola, *Sermons on Zachariah*, trans. C. E. Gilbert, [5], pp. 157–8.

DOCUMENT 27   COMPETING GUILDS

The above-mentioned consuls, assembled together in the palace of the [Wool] Guild ... have diligently considered the law approved by the captains of the Society of the blessed Virgin Mary of Orsanmichele. This law decreed, in effect, that for the ornamentation of that oratory, each of the twenty-one guilds of the city of Florence ... in a place assigned to each of them by the captains of the Society, should construct ... a tabernacle, properly and carefully decorated, for the honour of the city and the beautification of the oratory. The consuls have considered that all of the guilds have finished their tabernacles, and that those constructed by the Cloth and Banking Guilds, and by other guilds, surpass in beauty and ornamentation that of the Wool Guild. So it may truly be said that this does not redound to the honour of the Wool Guild, particularly when one considers the magnificence of that guild which always sought to be the master and the superior of the other guilds.

For the spendour and honour of the Guild, the lord consuls desire to provide a remedy for this ... They decree that ... the existing lord consuls ... are to construct, fabricate and remake a tabernacle and a statue of the blessed Stephen ... by whatever ways and means they choose, which will most honourably contribute to the splendour of the Guild, so that this tabernacle will exceed, or at least equal, in beauty and decoration the more beautiful ones. In the construction of this tabernacle and statue, the lord consuls ... may spend ... up to 1,000 florins.

Deliberation of the Consuls of the Wool Guild, 1425, trans. G. Brucker, *The Society of Renaissance Florence*, New York, 1971, pp. 93–4.

DOCUMENT 28   COMPETING ARTISTS

At that moment my friends wrote to me that the Board of Works of the temple of St John the Baptist [the baptistery] was sending for experienced masters, of whom they wanted to see a test piece. A great many well-qualified masters came from all over Italy to put themselves to this test and competition ... To each was given four bronze plates. The test set by the Board of Works was that everyone should do a scene for the doors; the one they chose was the Sacrifice of Isaac and they wanted each of the contestants to do the same scene ... To me was conceded the palm of victory by all the experts and by all my fellow competitors. Universally, they conceded to me the glory, without exception. Everyone felt I had surpassed the others in that time, without a single exception, after great consultation and examination by learned men. The Board of Works wanted to have their decision written out in their own hand; they were very expert men, including painters and sculptors in gold and silver and marble. There were thirty-four judges, counting those from the city and the surrounding areas; they all endorsed the victory in my favour – the consuls, the Board and all the members of the Merchants' Guild, which has the temple of St John the Baptist in its charge.

Lorenzo Ghiberti, *I Commentari*, ed. O. Morisani, Naples, 1947, p. 42; cf. [5], p. 84, and E. G. Holt, *A Documentary History of Art*, I, New York, 1957, pp. 157–8.

DOCUMENT 29   THE INFLUENCE OF ANCIENT MODELS

Your letters were most welcome for more than one reason, and I was particularly pleased to hear that my Lord [Sigismondo Malatesta, Lord of Rimini] was doing as I had hoped he would, and taking good counsel with everyone. But as for what you tell me Manetto [Antonio Manetti] says about cupolas having to be twice as high as they are wide, I for my part have more faith in those who built the Terme and the Pantheon and all those noble edifices, than in him, and a great deal more in reason than in any man. And if he bases himself on opinion, I shall not be surprised if he often makes mistakes.

I have also heard in the last day or two that Your Lordship [Lodovico Gonzaga, Marquis of Mantua] and your citizens have been discussing the building scheme here at Sant' Andrea. And that the principal intention was to have a great space where many people might go to behold the Blood of Christ. I saw Manetti's model. I liked it. But it did not seem the right thing to realise your intention. I thought it over and devised what I am sending you. This will be more practical, more immortal, more worthy and more gladdening. It will cost much less. This form of temple the Ancients called Sacred Etruscan. If you like it, I will do a correct version in proportion.

Leon Battista Alberti, letters to Matteo de' Pasti in Rimini, 18 November 1454, and to Lodovico Gonzaga in Mantua, *c.* 1470, trans. D. S. Chambers, [3], pp. 181–2, 113–14.

DOCUMENT 30   AUTHENTICITY AND THE ARTIST'S HAND

Master Leonardo – Hearing that you are staying in Florence, we have conceived the hope that something we have long desired might come true: to have something by your hand. When you were here and drew our portrait in charcoal, you promised one day to do it in colour. But because this would be almost impossible, since it would be inconvenient for you to move here, we beg you to keep your good faith with us by substituting for our portrait another figure even more acceptable to us: that is, to do a youthful Christ of about twelve years old, which would be the age he was when he disputed with the doctors in the Temple, and executed with that sweetness and soft ethereal charm which is the peculiar excellence of your art. If we are gratified by you in this strong desire of ours, you shall know that beyond the payment, which you yourself shall fix, we shall remain so obliged to you that we shall think of nothing else but to do you good service, and from this very moment we offer ourselves to act at your convenience and pleasure. Expecting a favourable reply we offer ourselves to do all your pleasure.

Isabella d'Este to Leonardo da Vinci, 14 May 1504, trans. D. S. Chambers, [3], p. 147.

DOCUMENT 31   ART CONNOISSEURSHIP

Sandro di Botticelli, a most excellent painter in panel and fresco, his things have a manly air and also have very good organization and complete balance.

Filippino da Fra Filippo, very good, pupil of the above, and son of the most remarkable master of his time, his things have a gentler air, I don't think they have as much skill.

Perugino, an outstanding master, especially in fresco, his things have an angelic air, very gentle.

Domenico di Ghirlandaio, good master in panel and more in fresco, his things have a good air, and he is very expeditious and does a lot of work.

All these above-named painters proved themselves in the Sistine Chapel except Filippino, but all of them at the Ospedaletto of Lord Lorenzo [Lorenzo de' Medici's villa at Spedaletto] and the choice is almost even.

Report from Florence to the Duke of Milan, *c.* 1490, trans. C. E. Gilbert, [5], p. 139.

DOCUMENT 32   THE TRADE IN FOREIGN ART

The painted papers, or rather canvases, I got two months ago, and you have been notified in several of my letters, and I gave Jacopo his as you had asked me several times. He seemed to like it quite well, and made us great offers. The other I have at home.

As to the two painted canvases, one is the Three Magi, offering gold to our Lord and they are good figures. The other is a peacock, which seems very fine to me, and is enriched with other decorations. To me they seem beautiful; I will keep one, because, from what you in your letter say they cost, I don't know if here one would get three florins apiece, for they are small canvases. If I had a chance to sell them at a profit, I would sell them both. The Holy Face I will keep, for it is a devout figure and beautiful.

Alessandra Strozzi to her son in Bruges, 1460, trans. C. E. Gilbert, [5], pp. 117–18.

CHANGING FASHIONS OR CHANGING VALUES?

DOCUMENT 33   ITALY *Á LA MODE* IN ENGLAND

It is the fashion of Italy, and especially of Naples (which is one of the richest parts of it) that all the Gentry dwell in the principall Towns, so the whole country is emptie. Even so now in England, all the country is gotten into London, so as with time, England will onely be London and the whole country be left waste ... So have wee got up the Italian fashion, in living miserably in our houses and dwelling all in the Citie: let us in Gods Name leave these idle forreine toyes and keepe the old fashion of England ...

And now out of my own mouth I declare unto you (which being in this place is equall to a proclamation which I intend likewise shortly hereafter to have publikely proclaimed) that only Courtiers, Citizens and Lawyers can stay in London ... And for the decrease of new Building here, I would have the builders restrained and committed to prison and if the builders cannot be found then the workmen to be imprisoned ... I mean such buildings as may be overthrown without inconvenience.

James I, speech in Star Chamber, 1616, *The Political Works of James I*, Cambridge, Mass., 1918, p. 343.

DOCUMENT 34   CHRISTIANITY AND PATRIOTISM

Considering, therefore, why it is that in ancient times the people were greater lovers of liberty than in our own times, I believe this arises from the same cause that makes men less strong today – and this, I believe, is due to the difference between our education and ancient education, based upon the difference between our religion and ancient religion. Since our religion has shown us the truth and the true path, it makes us value the honour of this world less; whereas the pagans, who valued it very much and considered it the highest good, were more fierce in their actions. This can be seen in many of their institutions, beginning with the magnificence of their sacrifices as compared with the meagreness of our own ... Besides this, ancient religion glorified only men who were endowed with worldly glory, such as generals of armies and rulers of republics; our religion has glorified humble and contemplative men rather than active ones. Furthermore, it has established as the supreme good humility, abjection, and contempt for human affairs, while ancient religion defined it as grandeur of spirit, strength of body, and all the other things likely to make men most vigorous. If it is true that our religion also requires strength, it is the kind of strength that makes you willing to suffer rather than to undertake bold deeds.

So this way of living, then, seems to have rendered the world weak and handed it over as prey to wicked men ... For if they would consider that religion permits us to defend and better the fatherland, they would see that it intends us to love and honour it and to prepare ourselves to be the kind of men who can defend It.

Niccolo Machiavelli, *The Discourses*, II, 2, trans. P. Bondanella and M. Musa, *The Portable Machiavelli*, London, 1953, pp. 297–9.

DOCUMENT 35   CHRISTIAN CONSCIENCE AND REASON OF STATE

I would go on to say that anyone who wants to hold dominions and states in this day and age should show mercy and kindness where possible, and where there is no other alternative, one must use cruelty and unscrupulousness. For this reason your great-uncle Gino wrote in those last memoirs of his [Gino Capponi, *Ricordi*] that it was necessary to appoint as members of the Ten of War people who loved their country more than their soul, because it is impossible to control governments and states, if one wants to hold them as they are held today, according to the precepts of Christian law ...

You see the position to which someone who wanted to govern states strictly according to conscience would be reduced. Therefore when I talked of murdering or keeping the Pisans imprisoned, I didn't perhaps talk as a Christian: I talked according to the reason and practice of states. Nor will anyone be more of a Christian who rejects such cruelty but recommends doing every-thing possible to take Pisa, since this means in effect being the cause of infinite evils to occupy something which doesn't according to conscience belong to you. Anyone who doesn't acknowledge this has no excuse before God, because – as the friars like to say – it shows 'crass ignorance' ... anyone who wants to live totally according to God's will can ill afford not to remove him-self totally from the affairs of this world, and it is difficult to live in the world without offending God.

You cannot hold states according to conscience. For if you consider their origin, they are all illegitimate, with the exception only of republics ruling their own cities, and nowhere else. Nor do I exempt the Emperor from this rule – and even less priests, for their violence is double, since they force us with temporal weapons and with spiritual ones.

Francesco Guicciardini, *Dialogue on the Government of Florence* and *Maxim* 48, trans. A. Brown [18], pp. 158–9, 172.

DOCUMENT 36 HUMANITY AND THE GROWTH OF
TOLERANCE

Mixing with the world has a marvellously clarifying effect on a man's judg-ment. We are all confined and pent up within ourselves, and our sight has contracted to the length of our own noses. When someone asked Socrates of what country he was he did not reply, 'of Athens', but 'of the world'. His was a fuller and wider imagination; he embraced the whole world as his city and extended his acquaintance, his society, and his affections to all mankind; unlike us, who look only under our own feet ...

I do not believe, from what I have been told about this people [cannibals from Brazil], that there is anything barbarous or savage about them, except that we all call barbarous anything that is contrary to our own habits ... I am not so anxious that we should note the horrible savagery of these acts, as con-cerned that whilst judging their faults so correctly we should be so blind to our own. I consider it more barbarous to eat a man alive than to eat him dead; to tear by rack and torture a body still full of feeling, to roast it by degrees, and then give it to be trampled and eaten by dogs and swine – a prac-tice which we have not only read about but seen within recent memory, not between ancient enemies, but between neighbours and fellow-citizens, and, what is worse, under the cloak of piety and religion – than to roast and eat a man after he is dead.

Michel de Montaigne, *Essays*, trans. J. M. Cohen, London (Penguin), 1958, I, 26 (On the Education of Children), and I, 31 (On Cannibals), pp. 63, 108, 113.

DOCUMENT 37   BARBARIANS AND THE NEW WORLD

They observe most barbarous customs in their eating; indeed, they do not take their meals at any fixed hours, but eat whenever they are so inclined, whether it be day or night. At meals they recline on the ground and do not use either tablecloths or napkins, being entirely unacquainted with linen and other kinds of cloth. The food is served in earthen pots which they make themselves, or else in receptacles made out of half-gourds ... In their sexual intercourse they have no legal obligations. In fact, each man has as many wives as he covets, and he can repudiate them later whenever he pleases, without it being considered an injustice or disgrace, and the women enjoy the same rights as the men. The men are not very jealous; they are, however, very sensual. The women are even more so than the men. I have deemed it best (in the name of decency) to pass over in silence their many arts to gratify their insatiable lust [*omitting a passage which in Latin describes how their husbands are made into eunuchs by being overexcited by their libidinous wives*] ...

    No one of this race, as far as we saw, observed any religious law. They can not justly be called either Jews or Moors; nay, they are far worse than the gentiles themselves or the pagans, for we could not discover that they performed any sacrifices nor that they had any special places or houses of worship. Since their life is so entirely given over to pleasure, I should style it Epicurean.

Amerigo Vespucci, *The First Voyage*, translated in *Cosmographiae Introductio*, 1607, repr. New York, 1969, p. 95; the original edition in Latin (Rome, 1502?) is reprinted in *Prime relazioni di navigatori italiani sulla scoperta dell'America. Colombo – Vespucci – Verazzano*, Turin, 1966, p. 88.

DOCUMENT 38   TRAVEL AND A DEBATE ABOUT GAMBLING

[*The description of a very cold and snowy night spent near Innsbruck, in a room shared by Vettori, his two companions (one religious 'and perhaps a hypocrite', the other 'not very religious') and also their servants, who were playing at cards to pass the night away. His friends' debate about gambling, because it was 'long, enjoyable and perhaps not without value', Vettori decided to include in his travel journal in the form of a dialogue.*]

Antonio I have often been surprised by some men's passion for gambling – despite being considered sensible and prudent; and by their excuse that they do it to avoid boredom and to pass the time away with as little bother as possible. I may be mistaken about a lot of things, but in this matter I shall be bold enough to state my mind. I think that, no matter who engages in it, gambling is as pernicious a vice as any you can find. Princes who suffer from it set a bad example to their subjects and waste the time that they should devote to thinking about governing and listening to those in need – and this leads to innumerable disasters. Nobles given over to this vice let everything go. Rich merchants become impoverished and poor ones become destitute. Young men who begin by winning become extravagant and lustful, and if they begin to lose, lose not only their money but also their character, becoming worthless and fraudulent instead of the fine men they could have been. Poor artisans consume on gambling both the time and the money that should have fed their families; peasants stop working the land. And so this cursed vice leads to all the disorders one could possibly imagine.

Venafro You will think my reply is too long, but it's impossible to confute your effective and subtle argument in a few words. I shall begin with a pre-supposition: that everything we do in this life, we do for the sake of pleasure. We can see this from our everyday experience. Beginning with those who are devoted Christians and live in fear of God, their only objective is pleasure, because they are – quite rightly – convinced that once the soul is liberated from the body, it will enjoy a life of celestial bliss and unimaginable happiness before it is rejoined with the body to live for ever in peace and joy.

The men who live worldly lives pursue pleasure in different ways. Some are ambitious, some love food and drink, some sexual pleasure, and some love amassing money. Some seek pleasure through bringing up their families well, or through their charity towards the poor and putting the public good before their own.

If this is the case and there is no single source of pleasure, how can we possibly criticise gambling? It prevents us suffering mental or physical anguish, it distracts us from the pleasures of the body and sex, from avarice, from cruelty and from all the shortcomings we are prone to. And even if it is the cause of many mistakes, doctors say that no medicine is so beneficial that it doesn't do some harm. Wine taken with moderation is beneficial, but if taken in excess, it is harmful, so gambling has many drawbacks but they result from it being abused. Sexual intercourse enables the human race to be maintained but is to be criticised when indulged in to excess; eating keeps the body alive but someone who never stops eating would be considered a beast. For this reason, we shouldn't condemn gambling out of hand, but only those who gamble without limit or restraint.

Francesco Vettori, *Viaggio in Alamagna,* [29], pp. 130–2.

BIBLIOGRAPHY

PRIMARY SOURCES

Collections of documents

1   *The Portable Renaissance Reader* , Penguin, London, 1953.
2   Cassirer, E., Kristeller, P. O. and Randall, J. H. (eds), *The Renaissance Philosophy of Man* , Chicago and London, 1948.
3   Chambers, D. S. (ed.), *Patrons and Artists in the Italian Renaissance*, London, 1970.
4   Cochrane, E. and Kirshner, J. (eds), *The Renaissance*, Chicago, 1986.
5   Gilbert, C. E. (ed.), *Italian Art, 1400–1500. Sources and Documents*, Englewood Cliffs, NJ, 1980.
6   Ross, Janet (ed.), *Lives of the Early Medici as told in their Correspondence*, London, 1910.

Single works

7   Alberti, Leon Battista, *On the family*, trans. R. N. Watkins as *The Family in Renaissance Florence*, Columbia University Press, New York, 1969; another translation in [4], pp.78–104.
8   Alberti, Leon Battista, *On painting* and *On sculpture*, ed. and trans. C. Grayson, London, 1972.
9   Ascham, R., *The Scholemaster*, 1570, ed. L. V. Ryan, Ithaca, NY, 1967.
10 Bodin, Jean, *The Six Bookes of a Commonweale*, trans. R. Knolles, 1606, reprinted 1962; abridged version by M. J. Tooley, Oxford, 1967.
11 Bracciolini, Poggio, *Letters*, trans. P. W. G. Gordan, *Two Renaissance Book Hunters. The Letters of Poggius Bracciolini to Nicolaus de Niccolis*, New York and London, 1974.
12 Bruni, Leonardo, *Dialogues to Pier Paulo Vergerio*, trans. in *The Three Crowns of Florence*, eds. D. Thompson and A. F. Nagel, New York, 1972, pp.19–52; 'On the constitution of the Florentines' in [4], pp.140–4.

13   Bruni, Leonardo, *Laudatio*, trans. in *The Earthly Republic*, eds. B. G. Kohl and R. G. Witt, Manchester, 1978, pp.135–75.

14   Elyot, Sir Thomas, *The Book Named the Governor*, London, 1962.

15   Erasmus, Desiderius, *The Praise of Folly*, trans. H. H. Hudson, Princeton, NJ, 1941.

16   Ficino, Marsilio, *The Letters*, a selection, 5 vols, London, 1975.

17   Gardiner, Stephen, *A Machiavellian Treatise*, ed. P. S. Donaldson, Cambridge, 1975.

18   Guicciardini, Francesco, *Dialogue on the Government of Florence*, trans. A. Brown, Cambridge, 1994.

19   Guicciardini, Francesco, *Maxims and Reflections (Ricordi)*, trans. M. Domandi, Philadelphia, 1965.

20   Machiavelli, Niccolo, *The Discourses*, ed. B.Crick, trans. L. J. Walker, London (Penguin), 1970.

21   Machiavelli, *Lettere*, ed. F. Gaeta, Milan, 1961.

22   Machiavelli, *The Prince*, trans. M. Bull, London (Penguin), 1961.

23   Medici, Lorenzo de', 'Novella di Giacoppo' in *Opere*, ed. E. Bigi, Turin, 1995, pp.603–18.

24   Melancthon, P., 'In laudem novae scholae', *Werke*, III, Tubingen, 1961.

25   Rabelais, F., *Gargantua and Pantagruel*, trans. J. M. Cohen, London (Penguin), 1955.

26   Rucellai, Giovanni, *Memoirs*, ed. A. Perosa, *Giovanni Rucellai e il suo Zibaldone*, London, 2 vols, I (text), 1960, II, 1981.

27   Vasari, Giorgio, *Le vite de' più eccellenti pittori, sculptori e architettori*, ed. R. Bettarini and P. Barocchi, Florence, 1967; trans. Everyman, London, 1963, 4 vols; abridged by G. Bull in Penguin Classics as *Lives of the Artists*, London, 1965.

28   Vespasiano da Bisticci, *Le vite*, ed. A. Greco, 2 vols, Florence, 1970–76, trans. W. G. and E. Waters, *Renaissance Princes, Popes and Prelates*, New York, 1963.

29   Vettori, Francesco, 'Viaggio in Alamagna', *Scritti storici e politici*, ed. E. Niccolini, Bari, 1972, pp.13–132.

SECONDARY SOURCES

30   Baron, H., *The Crisis of the Early Italian Renaissance*, 2nd edn, Princeton, NJ, 1966, criticised (with Baron's reply) by J. E. Seigel, *Past and Present* 34 (1966) and 36 (1967).

31   Baxandall, M., *The Limewood Sculptors of Renaissance Germany*, New Haven and London, 1980.

32   Benson, R. L. and Constable, G. (eds), *Renaissance and Renewal in the Twelfth Century*, Oxford, 1982.

33   Billanovich, G., 'Petrarch and the textual tradition of Livy', *Journal of the Warburg and Courtauld Institutes* 14 (1951), pp.137–208.

34   Black, Robert, 'The Donation of Constantine: A New Source for the Concept of the Renaissance?' in [38], pp.51–85.

35   Brotton, Jerry, *Trading Territories. Mapping the early modern world*, London, 1997.

36   Brown, Alison, 'De-civilizing the Renaissance', *Bulletin of the Society for Renaissance Studies* 15 (1997): 4–12.

37   Brown, Alison, *The Medici in Florence. The exercise and language of power*, Florence, 1992.

38   Brown, Alison (ed.), *Language and Images of Renaissance Italy*, Oxford, 1995.

39   Brown, Judith, 'Prosperity or hard times in Renaissance Italy', *Renaissance Quarterly* 42 (1989): 761–80.

40   Brown, J. C. and Davis, R. C. (eds), *Gender and Society in Renaissance Italy*, London, 1998.

41   Brown, Patricia Fortini, '*Renovatio* or *Conciliatio*? How Renaissances happened in Venice', in [38], pp.127–54.

42   Brown, Patricia Fortini, *Venice and Antiquity. The Venetian Sense of the Past*, New Haven and London, 1996.

43   Brucker, Gene, 'Humanism, politics and the social order in early Renaissance Florence', *Florence and Venice: Comparisons and Relations*, I (*Quattrocento*), Florence, 1979, pp.1–11.

44   Burckhardt, Jacob, *The Civilisation of the Renaissance in Italy*, Basle, 1860, trans. S. G. C. Middlemore, London, 1950.

45   Burke, Peter, 'Anthropology of the Italian Renaissance', *Journal of the Institute of Romance Studies* 1 (1992): 207–15.

46   Burke, Peter, *The Fortunes of the Courtier. The European Reception of Castiglione's* Cortigiano, Oxford, 1995.

47   Burke, Peter, *The Renaissance Sense of the Past*, London, 1969.

48   Burns, H., 'The Gonzaga and Renaissance architecture', in [50], pp.27–38.

49   Carrai, S., 'Implicazioni cortegiane nel' "Orfeo" di Poliziano', *Rivista della Letteratura Italiana* 8 (1990): 9–23.

50   Chambers, D. and Martineau, J. (eds), *Splendours of the Gonzaga*, London, 1981.

51   Chartier, R., *Cultural History. Between Practices and Representations*, Oxford, 1988.

52   Chartier, R., *The Order of Books*, Cambridge, 1994.

53   Chrisman, M. U., *Lay Culture. Learned Culture. Books and Social Change in Strasbourg, 1480–1599*, New Haven and London, 1982.

54   Cohen, T. V. and E. S., *Words and Deeds in Renaissance Rome: Trials before the Papal Magistrates*, Toronto, 1993.

55   Cohn, S. J., *The Cult of Remembrance and the Black Death*, Baltimore, 1992.

56   Cole, Alison, *Art of the Italian Renaissance Courts*, London, 1995.

57   Curtius, E. R., *European Literature and the Latin Middle Ages*, New York and Evanston, 1963.

58   Davies, Martin, *Columbus in Italy*, London (British Library), 1991.

59   Davies, Martin, *Aldus Manutius. Printer and Publisher of Renaissance Venice*, London (British Library), 1995.

60   Davies, Martin, 'Humanism in script and print in the fifteenth century', in [102], pp.47–62.

61   Davis, R. C., *The War of the Fists: Popular Culture and Public Violence in Late Renaissance Venice*, Oxford, 1994.

62   Debus, A. G., *Man and Nature in the Renaissance*, Cambridge, 1978.

63   De Certeau, M., *The Mystic Fable*, I, Chicago, 1992.

64   Edgerton, S. Y., *The Renaissance Rediscovery of Linear Perspective*, New York, 1976.

65   Eisenstein, E. L., *The Printing Revolution in Early Modern Europe*, Cambridge, 1983.

66   Elam, Caroline, 'Mantegna at Mantua', in [50], pp.15–25.

67   Elam, Caroline, 'Art and diplomacy in Renaissance Italy', *Journal of the Royal Society for the Arts* 136 (1988): 813–26.

68   Elias, Norbert, *The Civilising Process*, I (The History of Manners), 1939, trans., Oxford, 1978.

69   Findlen, Paula, *Possessing Nature. Museums, Collecting, and Scientific Culture in Early Modern Italy*, Berkeley, 1994.

70   Fletcher, J. M., 'Isabella d'Este, patron and collector' in [50], pp.51–63.

71   Foister, S., 'Tudor collections and collectors', *History Today* 35 (1985): 20–6.

72   Franz, D. O., *Festum Voluptatis. A Study of Renaissance Erotica*, Columbus, Ohio, 1989.

73   Gilbert, Creighton, 'What did the Renaissance patron buy?', *Renaissance Quarterly* 51 (1998): 392–450.

74   Gilbert, Felix, *The Pope, his Banker, and Venice*, Cambridge, Mass., 1980.

75   Goldberg, J. (ed.), *Queering the Renaissance*, Durham, NC, 1994.

76   Goldthwaite, R. A., *Wealth and the Demand for Art in Italy, 1300–1600*, Baltimore, 1993.

77   Gombrich, E. H., 'From the revival of letters to the reform of the arts', *Essays Presented to Rudolf Wittkower*, London, 1967, pp.71–82.

78   Gombrich, E. H., *In Search of Cultural History*, Oxford, 1969.

79   Gombrich, E. H., *Norm and Form*, London, 1971, esp. 'The early Medici as patrons of Art', pp.35–57, and 'Renaissance and Golden Age', pp.29–34.

80   Gombrich, E. H., 'The Renaissance – period or movement?', in [150], pp.9–30.

81   Grafton, Anthony, *Commerce with the Classics: Ancient Books and Renaissance Readers*, Ann Arbor, 1997.

82   Grafton, Anthony, *Joseph Scaliger. A Study in the History of Classical Scholarship*, I, Oxford, 1983.

83   Grafton, Anthony, *New Worlds, Ancient Texts. The Power of Tradition and the Shock of Discovery*, Cambridge, Mass., 1992.

84   Grafton, Anthony (ed.), *Rome Reborn. The Vatican Library and Renaissance Culture*, Washington and New Haven, 1993, at pp.3–46: 'The Vatican and its library'.

85   Grafton, A. and Jardine, L., *From Humanism to the Humanities. Education and the Liberal Arts in Fifteenth- and Sixteenth-Century Europe*, Duckworth, 1986.

86   Greenblatt, Stephen, *Marvelous Possessions. The Wonder of the New World*, Oxford, 1998.

87   Greenblatt, Stephen, *Renaissance Self-fashioning. From More to Shakespeare*, Chicago, 1984.

88   Greenblatt, Stephen, *Shakespearean Negotiations. The Circulation of Social Energy in Renaissance England*, Oxford, 1990.

89   Haines, Margaret, *The 'Sacrestia delle Messe' of the Florentine Cathedral*, Florence, 1983.

90   Holmes, G., *The Florentine Enlightenment*, London, 1969.

91   Jardine, Lisa, *Erasmus, Man of Letters. The Construction of Charisma in Print*, Princeton, 1993.

92   Jardine, Lisa, ' "O decus Italia Virgo". The myth of the learned lady in the Renaissance', *Historical Journal* 28 (1985): pp.799–819. See also [85].

93   Jardine, Lisa, *Worldly Goods. A New History of the Renaissance*, London, 1996.

94   Jones, Philip, *The Italian City-State. From Commune to Signoria*, Oxford, 1997.

95   Kelley, D. R., *The Foundation of Modern Historical Scholarship. Language, Law and History in the French Renaissance*, New York, 1970.

96   Kelley, Joan, 'Did women have a Renaissance?' in *Becoming Visible: Women in European History*, 2nd edition, eds R. Bridenthal, C. Koonz and S. Stuard, Boston, Mass., 1987, pp.175–201.

97   Kemp, Martin, *Behind the Picture. Art and Evidence in the Italian Renaissance*, New Haven and London, 1997.

98   Kent, F. W., 'The making of a Renaissance patron of the arts', in [26], II, pp.9–95.

99   Kent, F. W., 'Palaces, politics and society in fifteenth-century Florence', *I Tatti Studies*, 2 (1987): 41–70.

100 Kent, F. W. and Simons, P. (eds), *Patronage, Art and Society in Renaissance Italy*, Oxford, 1987.

101 Kohl, B. G. and Smith A. A., *Major Problems in the History of the Italian Renaissance*, Lexington, 1995.

102 Kraye, Jill (ed.), *The Cambridge Companion to Renaissance Humanism*, Cambridge, 1996.

103 Kristeller, P. O., *Renaissance Thought*, New York, 1961, pp.3–23; *Renaissance Thought II*, New York, 1965, pp.1–19.

104 Landau, David and Parshall, Peter, *The Renaissance Print, 1470–1550*, New Haven and London, 1944.

105 Larner, John, *Culture and Society in Italy, 1290–1420*, London, 1971.

106 Lenzuni, A. (ed.), *All' Ombra del Lauro. Documenti librari della cultura in età Laurenziana*, Florence, 1992.

107 Letts, R. M., *The Renaissance* (Cambridge Introduction to the History of Art), Cambridge, 1981.

108 Lopez, R., 'Hard times and investment in culture', reprinted in *The Renaissance: Six Essays*, New York and Evanston, 1962, pp.29–54.

109 Lowry, Martin, *The World of Aldus Manutius. Business and Scholarship in Renaissance Venice*, Oxford, 1978.

110 Marsh, David, trans. Leon Battista Alberti, *Dinner Pieces*, Binghamton, 1987.

111 Meiss, Millard, *Painting in Florence and Siena after the Black Death*, Princeton, 1951.

112 Menocai, M. R., *Shards of Love. Exile and the Origins of the Lyric*, Durham and London, 1994.

113 Molho, A., 'Cosimo de' Medici: *Pater Patriae* or *Padrino?*', *Stanford Italian Review* (1979): 5–33.

114 Najemy, John, 'The dialogue of power in Florentine politics' in *Cities and City-States in Classical Antiquity and Medieval Italy*, eds Molho, A. *et al.*, Stuttgart and Ann Arbor, 1991, pp.269–88.

115 Najemy, John, 'The Republic's two bodies: body metaphors in Italian Renaissance political thought' in [38], pp.237–62.

116 Nauert, C. G., *Humanism and the Culture of Renaissance Europe*, Cambridge, 1995.

117 Nelson, Jonathan, 'An introduction to the life and styles of Filippino Lippi' in *The Drawings of Filippino Lippi and His Circle*, Exhibition Catalogue, Metropolitan Museum of Art, New York, 1997, pp.9–19.

118 Niccoli, Ottavia, *Prophecy and People in Renaissance Italy*, Princeton, 1990.

119 Norman, Diana (ed.), *Siena, Florence and Padua. Art, Society and Religion, 1280–1400*, I, New Haven and London, 1995.

120 Outram, Dorinda, *The Enlightenment*, Cambridge, 1995.

121 Panofsky, Erwin, *Renaissance and Renascences in Western Art*, 1972.

122 Piltz, Anders, *The World of Medieval Learning*, Oxford, 1981.

123 Porter, R. and Teich, M., *The Renaissance in National Context*, Cambridge, 1992.

124 Quint, David, 'Humanism and Modernity: a reconsideration of Bruni's dialogues', *Renaissance Quarterly* 38 (1985), pp.423–45.

125 Raab, F., *The English Face of Machiavelli*, London, 1964.

126 Radcliff-Umstead, D., *The Birth of Modern Comedy in Renaissance Italy*, Chicago, 1969.

127 Rahe, P. A., *Republics Ancient and Modern. Classical Republicanism and the American Revolution*, Chapel Hill, 1992.

128 Rebhorn, W. A., *Foxes and Lions. Machiavelli's Confidence Men*, Ithaca, NY, 1988.

129 Reynolds, L. D. and Wilson, N. G., *Scribes and Scholars. A Guide to the Transmission of Greek and Latin Literature*, 3rd edition, Oxford, 1991.

130 Rhodes, D. E., *Gli annali tipografici fiorentini del XV secolo*, Florence, 1988.

131 *La Rinascita della Scienza*, in the catalogue of the exhibition *Firenze e la Toscana dei Medici nell' Europa del Cinquecento'*, Florence, 1980, pp.123–308.

132 Rocke, Michael, *Forbidden Friendships: Homosexuality and Male Culture in Renaissance Florence*, New York, 1996.

133 Rubinstein, N., *The Government of Florence under the Medici (1434–1494)*, 2nd edition, Oxford, 1997.

134 Rubinstein, N., 'Political theories in the Renaissance', in *The Renaissance. Essays in Interpretation*, London, 1982, pp.153–200.

135 Ryan, Kiernan, *Shakespeare*, 2nd edition, London, 1995.

136 Santagata, Marco, *I frammenti dell'anima. Storia e racconto nel Canzoniere di Petrarca*, Bologna, 1993.

137 Saslow, J. M., *The Medici Wedding of 1589. Florentine Festival as* Theatrum Mundi, New Haven and London, 1996.

138 Sawday, Jonathan, *The Body Emblazoned. Dissection and the human body in Renaissance culture*, London, 1995.

139 Saxl, F., 'A Marsilio Ficino manuscript written in Bruges in 1475', *Journal of the Warburg and Courtauld Institutes* 1 (1937–38): 61–2.

140 Scholderer, Victor, *Printers and Readers in Italy in the Fifteenth Century*, London, 1949.

141 Simons, P., 'Portraiture, portrayal, and idealization: Ambiguous individualism in representations of Renaissance women', in [38], pp.263–311.

142 Skinner, Quentin, *The Foundations of Modern Political Thought* I (The Renaissance), II (The Age of Reformation), Cambridge, 1978.

143 Smith, Christine, *Architecture in the Culture of Early Humanism. Ethics, Aesthetics and Eloquence, 1400–1470*, New York and Oxford, 1992.

144 Southern, R. W., *Medieval Humanism and Other Studies*, Oxford, 1984.

145 Stillwell, M. B., *The Awakening Interest in Science During the First Century of Printing, 1450–1550*, New York, 1970.

146 Stratford, J., 'The Royal Collections to 1461', in *The Cambridge History of the Book in Britain*, eds. L. Hellinga and J. B. Trapp, Cambridge, 1999, pp. 255–66.

147 Strong, R., *Art and Power. Renaissance Festivals, 1450–1650*, Woodbridge, Suffolk, 1984.

148 Thompson, J. W., *The Medieval Library*, Chicago, 1939.

149 Thornton, Dora, *The Scholar in his Study. Ownership and Experience in Renaissance Italy*, New Haven and London, 1997.

150 Trapp, J. B. (ed.), *Background to the English Renaissance*, London, 1974, at pp.67–89, 'Education in the Renaissance'.

151 Trexler, R. C., *Public Life in Renaissance Florence*, New York and London, 1980.

152 Ventrone, Paola, *Gli araldi della commedia. Teatro a Firenze nel Rinascimento*, Pisa, 1993.

153 Verdon, T. (ed.) with J. Henderson, *Christianity and the Renaissance, Image and Religious Imagination in the Quattrocento*, Syracuse, 1990.

154 Waley, D., *The Italian City-Republics*, 2nd edition, London, 1978.

155 Weiss, R., *Humanism in England during the Fifteenth Century*, Oxford, 1957.

156 Weiss, R., *The Renaissance Discovery of Classical Antiquity*, Oxford, 1969.

157 Welch, E., *Art and Society in Italy, 1350–1500*, Oxford, 1997.

158 Wilkins, E. H., *Life of Petrarch*, Chicago and London, 1961.

159 Witt, R. G., 'The *De tyranno* and Coluccio Salutati's view of politics and Roman history', *Nuova Rivista Storica* 53 (1969): 434–74.

160 Wittkower, R., *Architectural Principles in the Age of Humanism*, London, 1962.

161 Woods-Marsden, J., 'Toward a history of art patronage in the Renaissance: the case of Pietro Aretino', *Journal of Medieval and Renaissance Studies* 24 (1994): 275–99.

162 Woodward, W. H., *Vittorino da Feltre and Other Humanist Educators*, Cambridge, 1897, reprinted New York, 1963.

163 Yates, F. A., *Giordano Bruni and the Hermetic Tradition*, London, 1964.

INDEX

THE RENAISSANCE